U0489060

義正閣 主编

西泠印社出版社

瓷器，作为中华传统文化瑰宝之一，其历史源远流长，尤其是瓷都景德镇烧制的官窑，制作精细，千娇百媚，千古流传。初识清瓷，我仅为其胎表面光洁如玉、造型精致典雅、图案色彩绚丽所吸引，随岁月流转，感悟日增，方知瓷器背后深厚的历史底蕴与文化魅力，慢慢走上穿越时空的收藏之路。

我涉足收藏始于偶然。二十年前在整理旧宅物品时，几件清代瓷器让我注目，一种难以言喻的欢喜使我爱不释手。风起于青蘋之末，感恩先辈的遗留对我的启发，打开了我与古董瓷器的缘分之门。此后闲暇时光，我拜读相关史籍，翻阅瓷器书刊，参观各地博物馆，留连古玩市场，结交专业人士，经过一段时间的沉淀，我走进了拍卖场参与瓷器竞拍。始于偶然之触发，终于耐久之深爱，古瓷的精湛艺术始终让我兴趣盎然，愉悦快活。

我收藏的持续动力还源于对明清官窑的着迷。我很难拒绝珍品的审美享受，陶醉于它们的魅力之中，心仪之物自收入囊中那一刻起便时时喜悦。古董是永恒的，能在这些历经沧桑的珍瓷上留下自己的一段缘分，我觉得很欣慰。

回忆起自己涉足拍场的多年时光，那次竞得清代藏品的经历仍记忆犹新。经过多轮竞价后获得的清代官窑珍品，更增添了我对收藏的热爱。当然我也尊重他人的缘分，与竞品失之交臂我也并不遗憾，视之为他人的机缘。古董不能分身，但只要你喜欢，与之有过这样一段曾想拥有的经历，那么它的精彩在记忆和回味中就不可抹去了。这让我更加坚信，真正的收藏不在于得失之间，而在于心中对那份美好的追求和珍惜，这何尝不是一件让人愉悦的事呢。

许多年过去了，我爱古瓷乐此不疲，常与朋友们共享古董的乐趣。也一直有朋友建议将收藏结集出版，我最终接受了他们的美意，愿与更多爱瓷人士一起来欣赏中华古瓷的精美绝伦。

衷心感谢帮助过我的亲朋好友，尤其感谢许多专业人士对我的真诚指点。我深信，瓷器收藏之旅必是长久而精彩的！

葛平义

2024 年 春

Delving into the world of China's porcelain heritage has been a fascinating journey, one that has connected me deeply with the intricate history and cultural significance of these artful creations. Jingdezhen's imperial kilns, a pinnacle of China's traditional crafts, are renowned for their impeccable artistry and enduring charm. My initial connection with Qing porcelain was drawn from its serene, jade-like surface, the elegance of its form, and the vibrancy of its colors. This initial admiration was the gateway to a deeper appreciation of its historical significance and cultural essence.

My venture into collecting began unexpectedly twenty years ago, while sorting through items in old family house, several Qing Dynasty porcelains caught my eye, sparking an indescribable joy and leading to repeated admirations. I am grateful to my ancestors for inspiring me and opening the door to my destiny with antique porcelain. My free time became filled with studying historical texts on porcelain, exploring museums, wandering through antique markets, and engaging with knowledgeable enthusiasts. This gradual immersion led me to the world of auctions, transforming a budding interest into a lifelong passion.

The continuous growth of my collection is driven by a fascination with the exquisite pieces from the Ming and Qing imperial kilns. Their aesthetic appeal is irresistibly captivating, and the charm they exude is deeply enchanting. Each addition to my collection brings a sense of joy and fulfillment. These timeless antiques, each with its own story etched by history, are not just possessions but markers of a journey through time.

Reflecting on my years in the auction world, the experience of acquiring a Qing Dynasty piece remains vivid in my memory. Securing a Qing Dynasty imperial kiln treasure after numerous rounds of bidding only fueled my passion for collecting. In auctions, my missed chances are not regrets but acknowledgments of the antiques' destined connection with others. Collectibles endure through time, but as long as you have liked it, and experienced such a desire to possess it, its brilliance will remain indelible in your memory and reflection. This has strengthened my belief that true collecting is not about gains or losses but rather cherishing and pursuing beauty, which is, in itself, comforting.

As time has passed, my love for ancient porcelain has only deepened. Sharing this passion with friends and enthusiasts has been a source of great joy. Inspired by their encouragement, I have compiled my collection into this publication, hoping to share the beauty of Chinese ancient porcelain with a wider audience.

I am deeply grateful to my friends, family, and the many professionals who have guided and supported me on this journey. I am confident that the path of porcelain collecting will continue to be a source of fascination and discovery.

Yizheng Collection
Spring 2024

明 *MING DYNASTY*

永乐 宣德 *YONGLE AND XUANDE PERIOD*

青花缠枝花卉纹花口盘 002
A BLUE AND WHITE BARBED "FLORAL" PLATE

青花折枝花果纹葵口碗 006
A BLUE AND WHITE LOBED "FRUIT AND FLOWER" BOWL

青花折枝花果纹大碗 008
A VERY RARE BLUE AND WHITE "FRUIT" BOWL

青花双莲瓣缠枝莲纹碗 010
A BLUE AND WHITE LOTUS BOWL

清 *QING DYNASTY*

康熙 *KANGXI PERIOD*

五彩《望月图》诗文笔筒 016
AN EXTRAORDINARY, FINE AND LARGE INSCRIBED FAMILLE-VERTE BRUSHPOT

釉里红加五彩花卉纹苹果尊 020
A RARE AND EXCEPTIONAL COPPER-RED AND FAMILLE-VERTE "ROSE" VASE

釉里红加五彩花卉纹马蹄尊 022
A FINE AND RARE ENAMELLED AND COPPER-RED DECORATED WATER POT, HORSESHOE VASE

冬青釉浅浮雕祥云纹马蹄式水盂 026
A FINE CARVED CELADON-GLAZED "CLOUD" WATER POT

青花海水云龙纹文具盒 028
A RARE BLUE AND WHITE "DRAGON" CALLIGRAPHY BOX WITH COVER

青花五彩八月桂花花神杯 030
A WUCAI "OSMANTHUS" MONTHLY CUP

青花五彩六月荷花花神杯 032
A RARE WUCAI "LOTUS" MONTHLY CUP

珊瑚红地瓷胎画珐琅九秋图宫碗 034
A FINE AND RARE CORAL-GROUND FAMILLE-VERTE FLORAL BOWL

青花斗绿彩赶珠云龙纹大盘 036
A FINE AND RARE GREEN-ENAMELLED "DRAGON" DISH

清 QING DYNASTY

雍正 YONGZHENG PERIOD

斗彩鸡缸杯 040
A RARE DOUCAI CHICKEN CUP

斗彩团菊纹杯 044
A FINE DOUCAI "CHRYSANTHEMUM MEDALLION" WINE CUP

斗彩暗八仙纹碗 046
A FINE DOUCAI "ANBAXIAN" BOWL

矾红夔凤纹水盂 048
A RARE IRON-RED DECORATED PHOENIX WATERPOT

柠檬黄釉茶圆一对 050
A PAIR OF VERY RARE YELLOW GLAZE BOWLS

松石绿釉葵式茶碗一对 052
A VERY RARE PAIR OF MOULDED TURQUOISE-ENAMELLED MALLOW-FORM TEA BOWLS

霁红釉小瓶 056
A RARE COPPER-RED GLAZED VASE

霁蓝釉胆瓶一对 060
A PAIR OF VERY RARE BOTTLE VASES WITH BLUE GLAZE

斗彩缠枝西番莲纹长颈瓶 062
A VERY RARE DOUCAI VASE WITH ENTWINED BRANCHES AND LOTUS DESIGN

窑变釉双耳盘口瓶 066
A VERY RARE VASE WITH FLAMBÉ GLAZE

洒蓝地白花缠枝花卉纹盘 070
A RARE REVERSE-DECORATED POWDER-BLUE "GARDENIA" DISH

青花加矾红折枝宝相花纹杯 072
A FINE UNDERGLAZE-BLUE AND IRON-RED "LOTUS" CUP

斗彩菊花捧寿纹盘 074
A FINE DOUCAI CHRYSANTHEMUM AND LONGEVITY PATTERN PLATE

斗彩海屋添筹图盘 076
A RARE DOUCAI "IMMORTALS" DISH

斗彩如意云龙纹盘 078
A VERY RARE DOUCAI "DRAGON" DISH

斗彩绿龙纹盘 080
A FINE AND RARE UNDERGLAZE-BLUE AND GREEN-ENAMELLED "DRAGON" DISH

釉里红三鱼纹盘一对 082
A FINE PAIR OF COPPER-RED DECORATED "THREE-FISH" DISHES

清 QING DYNASTY

乾隆 QIANLONG PERIOD

青花釉里红狮滚绣球纹尊 086
A FINE AND VERY RARE UNDERGLAZE-BLUE AND COPPER-RED "LION" VASE

青花缠枝番莲寿字纹如意尊 090
A FINE AND VERY RARE BLUE-AND-WHITE DOUBLE-GOURD VASE

青花双龙捧寿纹如意耳葫芦扁瓶一对 094
A PAIR OF BLUE AND WHITE DRAGON DOUBLE-GOURD VASES

粉彩云龙纹笔 096
A FINE AND RARE FAMILLE-ROSE "DRAGON" BRUSH

釉里红喜上眉梢图如意耳抱月瓶 098
A RARE UNDERGLAZE-RED "MAGPIE AND PRUNUS" MOONFLASK

胭脂红地洋彩轧道锦上添花纹贯耳扁瓶 100
A YANGCAI RUBY-GROUND SGRAFFITO LOTUS VASE

松绿地粉彩缠枝莲纹五子登科包袱瓶 102
A VERY RARE PINE TURQUOISE GROUND FAMILLE ROSE "FIVE SCHOLARS ATTAINING SCHOLARLY HONORS" POUCH-SHAPED VASE

粉彩仿掐丝珐琅番莲福寿纹双龙耳瓶 106
A VERY RARE FAMILLE-ROSE CLOISONNE-IMITATION BOTTLE VASE

仿雕漆珊瑚红地描金瑞蝠穿云游龙纹帽架 108
A VERY RARE IMITATION-LACQUER "DRAGON" PORCELAIN HAT STAND

粉青釉刻螭龙纹盘口纸槌瓶 110
A CELADON GLAZE "DRAGON" MALLET SHAPE VASE

粉青釉弦纹高足杯 112
A FINE STEMBOWL WITH PALE BLUISH-GREEN CELADON GLAZE

仿汝釉出戟花觚 114
A FINE RU-TYPE VASE, HUAGU

浆胎仿定釉暗刻兽面纹盖碗尊 116
A FINE AND RARE CREAMY-WHITE GLAZED SOFT-PASTE VASE

冬青釉刻缠枝牡丹纹长颈瓶 118
A RARE AND FINE CELADON ENAMELED PORCELAIN VASE WITH MOLDED DECORATION

仿官釉八卦琮式瓶 120
A FINE GE-TYPE GLAZED CONG-SHAPED VASE

炉钧釉灯笼瓶 122
A ROBIN'S-EGG BLUE GLAZED LANTERN VASE

青花八吉祥纹双龙耳抱月瓶 124
A SUPERB LARGE MING-STYLE BLUE AND WHITE "BAJIXIANG" MOONFLASK

青花折枝花卉纹六方瓶 128
AN EXCEPTIONALLY FINE AND MAGNIFICENT BLUE AND WHITE "SANDUO" HEXAGONAL VASE

青花缠枝西番莲团寿纹六方贯耳瓶 132
A FINE BLUE-AND-WHITE "LOTUS SCROLL" HEXAGONAL VASE

青花缠枝花卉纹铺首尊 134
A FINE BLUE AND WHITE "FLORAL" VASE

青花缠枝花卉开光福寿纹抱月瓶 136
A BLUE-AND-WHITE PEACH “MEDALLION” MOONFLASK

斗彩团菊纹盖罐 138
A DOUCAI “LOTUS AND CHRYSANTHEMUM” JAR AND COVER

暗刻海水绿龙盘 140
A GREEN-ENAMELED “DRAGON” DISH

松石绿地粉彩描金宝相花纹茶碗 142
A FINE TURQUOISE GROUND FAMILLE ROSE BOWL

清 QING DYNASTY

嘉庆 JIAQING AND 道光 DAOGUANG PERIOD

青花矾红云龙纹盖盒一对 146
A RARE PAIR OF BLUE AND WHITE “DRAGON” BOXES WITH COVERS

珊瑚红地五彩描金婴戏图碗 148
A RARE AND FINE CORAL-GROUND FAMILLE-ROSE “BOYS” BOWL

胭脂红地轧道洋彩开光五谷丰登图碗一对 150
A FINE PAIR OF RUBY-GROUND FAMILLE-ROSE SGRAFFIATO “LANTERNS” BOWLS

胭脂红地轧道洋彩开光四季山水纹碗 152
A FINE AND RARE RUBY-GROUND FAMILLE-ROSE SGRAFFIATO “LANDSCAPE” BOWL

蓝地轧道洋彩开光花卉纹碗 154
A RARE BLUE-GROUND FAMILLE-ROSE “MEDALLION” BOWL

粉地轧道洋彩开光丹桂玉兔纹碗一对 156
A FINE PAIR OF PINK-GROUND FAMILLE-ROSE “MEDALLION” BOWLS

黄地轧道洋彩开光花卉纹碗 158
A FINE YELLOW-GROUND FAMILLE-ROSE “MEDALLION” BOWL

黄地轧道洋彩开光山水纹碗 160
YELLOW-GROUND FAMILLE-ROSE “MEDALLION” BOWL

蓝地轧道洋彩牛郎织女图碗 162
A FINE BLUE-GROUND FAMILLE-ROSE 'MEDALLION' BOWL

胭脂红地轧道洋彩开光花果纹碗 164
A VERY FINE RUBY-GROUND GRAFFIATO “MEDALLION” BOWL

義正閣

YIZHENG GE PORCELAIN ALBUM

明 永乐 宣德

MING DYNASTY,
YONGLE AND XUANDE PERIOD

明 永乐

青花缠枝花卉纹花口盘 直径：33.5 厘米

是器口沿平出，呈十二出菱花式口。此种器型始见于元代，非中国传统瓷器式样，而与中亚陶器及金属制大盘极似，为明代永乐青花之典型器物。通体青花纹饰，外壁近口沿处饰弦纹、回纹，中间饰缠枝菊花纹一周。盘心绘牡丹花、茶花、莲花、石榴花、秋葵等诸式花卉纹；内、外壁绘十二朵折枝花、莲花、牡丹、菊花、牵牛花等六种形态各异的四季花卉；折沿绘一周缠枝灵芝纹，枝蔓卷曲叶片舒展自然，为西亚纹饰风格。纹饰写实传神，充分借鉴国画的笔墨意韵，得其法度，勾、勒、点、染诸法，运用皆宜。线条粗细并用，青料浓淡兼施，呈色极富层次，铁锈斑深入胎骨，画面颇具苍翠欲滴的意趣，透出凝重雄浑之美。

MING DYNASTY, YONGLE PERIOD

A BLUE AND WHITE BARBED "FLORAL" PLATE

Diameter: 33.5 cm

The plate's rim extends flatly, taking the shape of twelve bracket foliations. It traces its design origins to the Yuan Dynasty. It stands as a quintessential example of blue-and-white porcelain from the Yongle era of the Ming Dynasty. Decorated throughout with blue and white motifs, it showcases string and wave patterns near the rim, central floral designs, and twelve various blossoms with six different kinds on both inner and outer walls representing the four seasons. The intertwining lingzhi pattern on the rim reflects a West Asian influence. Drawing from traditional Chinese painting techniques, the plate's detailed artwork exhibits rich contrasts and depth, with deep iron oxide spots enhancing its lush and majestic beauty.

永遇樂
詠宣德青花折枝花果紋葵口碗

青青葵開　朱粉不施
萬般皆好
碗底仙桃　摘承金酒
勸千長壽
仙山流霞　東海吹沫
一捧與天同老
樽有葡萄簪有蓮
牡丹纏　石榴笑

明 宣德

青花折枝花果纹葵口碗 直径：22.7 厘米

大明宣德年制（六字双行楷书款）

是器敞口，呈六瓣葵口式，斗笠形，斜腹，圈足。全器内外纹饰疏朗而饱满，外壁饰两重纹样，上为六组折枝瑞果纹，下为六组折枝花卉纹，交错布置，内壁口沿缀饰十二式花果纹，下承六组折枝花卉纹与外壁纹饰相对应，碗心则绘以折枝寿桃纹。整器胎质细腻坚致，釉汁莹润亮青。

祥花瑞果为永宣青花经典纹饰，是器涵盖了祥花瑞果的诸多品类，如菊花、牡丹、莲花、茶花、蟠桃、枇杷、荔枝、石榴、葡萄、樱桃。其绘画写实逼真，诸花妍放生姿，众果饱满诱人。

敏求精舍旧藏

MING DYNASTY, XUANDE MARK AND PERIOD

A BLUE AND WHITE LOBED "FRUIT AND FLOWER" BOWL Diameter: 22.7 cm

This piece boasts an open six-petaled sunflower rim, a slanting body, and a ringed base. The bowl's decoration, both inside and out, is elegantly sparse yet full. The outer wall features two layers of patterns: the upper layer consists of six sets of fruit branches, and the lower displays six sets of floral branches, arranged alternately. At the bowl's heart is a longevity peach motif. The porcelain's fine texture complements its lustrous blue glaze. The base is inscribed Xuande six-character mark in underglaze blue.

The bowl epitomizes the classic blue and white motifs of the Yongle and Xuande periods, featuring diverse flowers and fruits such as peony, lotus, loquat, and cherry. The vivid portrayal of these elements attests to its lifelike artistry.

Collection of the Mingqiu Society

明 宣德

青花折枝花果纹大碗 直径：28 厘米

大明宣德年制（六字单行楷书款）

是器胎体厚重，釉质细腻，内施白釉，外壁通体青花装饰，口沿绘青花弦纹两道，腹部绘六组折枝花果纹：石榴、寿桃、荔枝、柿子、枇杷、葡萄，寓“多子多寿”之意。近足处绘莲瓣纹一周，圈足侧墙以梅花装饰，疏朗别致。其构图疏朗自然，虚实相济，无缠枝纹饰常见繁密局促之虞，笔触细腻，独显宣德青花之豪迈气概，深得水墨神髓。

此式为宣德一朝新出之款，造型敦实端庄，胎体厚重坚致，口沿平切，棱角明显，为宣德碗类最奇特者，能与之相当的品类，仅见洒蓝釉暗刻龙纹钵和青花云龙纹钵，皆以厚胎平口著称。

天民楼旧藏

MING DYNASTY, XUANDE MARK AND PERIOD

A VERY RARE BLUE AND WHITE "FRUIT" BOWL

Diameter: 28 cm

The interior of this bowl features a white glaze with no patterns, while the exterior is adorned with blue and white motifs. A detailed frieze encircles the body, depicting fruiting branches with symbols of longevity and prosperity such as peach, pomegranate, loquat, grape, persimmon, and litchi. This primary motif is framed by a double line bordering the mouth rim. Near the base, a band of upright lotus petal pattern adds further sophistication, leading down to the circular foot adorned with plum blossoms motifs, echoing the charm and finesse of Ming. The overall composition is naturally laid out with a perfect balance between filled and empty spaces. Without the usual clutter of intertwining patterns, the design showcases the delicate brushwork and captures the bold spirit of the Xuande blue and white porcelain, deeply rooted in the essence of ink painting. The Xuande six-character mark is inscribed in underglaze blue just below the exterior rim.

From the Xuande era, this style stands out with its robust form and unique flat-cut rim. Its distinctiveness is paralleled only by the blue-glazed dragon bowl and the blue and white cloud dragon pattern bowl, both renowned for their thick body and flat rim.

Collection of the Tianminlou Foundation

大明宣德年製

明 宣德

青花双莲瓣缠枝莲纹碗 直径：20.8 厘米

大明宣德年制（六字双行楷书款）

是器敞口，深弧壁，窄底，圈足，碗心内凹呈尖底状，底微凸，俗称“鸡心碗”，一般因其碗形颇似莲房，俗又称“莲子碗”。碗外壁青花绘双层莲瓣纹，口沿波涛纹一圈。内口沿回纹一圈，内壁绘缠枝莲花六朵，碗心为折枝石榴花果。全器胎质缜密坚硬，釉质润泽。纹饰描绘层次分明，繁而不乱，青花色泽艳丽。

宣德朝青花莲子碗，外壁分单层或双层莲瓣纹两款，源自永乐青花鸡心碗。碗心纹饰多为阿拉伯风格的花卉图案，外壁环单层花瓣。至宣德朝，碗心改以中国传统花果纹装饰，如本碗碗心饰石榴纹，结合莲花图案，寓意“连生贵子”。

此类碗式有浓厚的波斯风格，伊朗14世纪早期的陶碗其造型与外壁装饰纹样与此碗相类，或为其蓝本原型。而美索不达米亚的彩陶花纹盘的盘心亦常使用相似的放射性莲瓣纹装饰，可见传承。

陈玉阶旧藏

蝶戀花

詠宣德青花雙蓮瓣纏枝蓮紋碗

一掬瓊漿青粉膩
蓮子心中 自有深深意
明月藍花重疊砌
毛穎宛轉蓮纏枝

MING DYNASTY, XUANDE MARK AND PERIOD

A BLUE AND WHITE LOTUS BOWL Diameter: 20.8 cm

This bowl, commonly referred to as lianzi due to its resemblance to a lotus seed pod, is characterized by an open top, deep curved sides, and a pointed base that protrudes outward. The exterior is adorned with dual-toned blue and white motifs of lotus petals set below a cresting wave pattern along the rim. The interior is decorated with a key-fret pattern that encircles intertwined lotus flowers, converging on a central motif of a pomegranate spray. The bowl's lustrous glaze and vivid colors accentuate its elaborate designs.

Encircled by double rings, the base of the bowl is inscribed with Da Ming Xuande Nian Zhi (Made in the reign of Xuande in the Great Ming Dynasty), consisting of six characters in single column in regular script.

Lianzi bowls from the Xuande era, which feature either single or double layers of lotus designs, evolved from the smaller chicken-heart bowls of the Yongle period. These earlier bowls were distinguished by pointed centers and Arabesque floral patterns. During the Xuande period, there was a shift towards revamping traditional Chinese motifs such as the pomegranate and lotus, which symbolize prosperity and noble lineage, respectively.

The bowl exhibits significant Persian influences, suggesting that its design may have been inspired by 14th-century Iranian ceramics, potentially serving as its prototype. Moreover, the radial lotus petal decorations are reminiscent of the heart designs found on Mesopotamian polychrome pottery dishes, indicating a shared heritage.

Collection of Y.C. Chen

義正閣

YIZHENG GE PORCELAIN ALBUM

清 康熙

QING DYNASTY KANGXI PERIOD

清 康熙

五彩《望月图》诗文笔筒

直径：18.4 厘米

是器满绘《望月图》，传神捕捉文人对月遥想之雅韵诗情。器身并题王昌龄之名。王昌龄为唐代诗人，擅写塞外风光。笔筒题诗："听月楼高太清，南山对户分明。昨夜姮娥现影，嫣然笑里传声。莘野樵笔。"钤"汪""朱石居"印。此诗乃望月名篇，写景抒情并举，情景交融。如此尺寸硕大并加题诗之康熙五彩笔筒甚为罕见，所绘色彩明艳娇妍，笔触疏秀清润，人物形神俱佳。

康熙御瓷，多有取材自木刻版画之作，是器正属一例。所绘《望月图》及题诗源自黄风池（活跃于 17 世纪早期）所编《唐诗画谱》。题诗落款乃"莘野樵"，而现存并无有关莘氏之记载。杭州西湖博物馆收藏一五彩盘，亦带有"莘野樵"款，由此显示此人或为景德镇作坊艺匠，抑或为委托艺匠烧制瓷笔筒之人，所作极为珍罕。

洁蕊堂旧藏

著录于杰弗里·施塔门、辛西娅·沃尔克、倪亦斌编：《文采卓然：洁蕊堂藏康熙盛世瓷》，布鲁日，2017 年，图版 30。

QING DYNASTY, KANGXI PERIOD

AN EXTRAORDINARY, FINE AND LARGE INSCRIBED FAMILLE-VERTE BRUSHPOT

Diameter: 18.4 cm

Elegantly enameled with the "moon-gazing" scene, this brushpot masterfully captures the poetic essence of literati's distant contemplation of the moon. The brushpot bears a poem "moon-gazing" by Wang Changling, a renowned Tang dynasty poet acclaimed for his portrayal of frontier landscapes. Stamped with "Wang" and "Zhu Shi Ju" seals. This moon-gazing masterpiece exudes both evocative landscapes and deep emotions, blending scenery and sentiment seamlessly. Such a large Kangxi famille-verte brushpot, with its vibrant colors, graceful brushwork, and lifelike figures, is truly a rarity.

This Kangxi imperial porcelain often drew inspiration from woodblock prints, with this piece being no exception. The depicted moon-gazing scene and accompanying poem originate from the Illustrations to Tang poems by Huang Fengchi (active in the early 17th century). The poem is inscribed "Xin Yeqiao", but there is no record of such person. However, a famille-verte plate collected by the West Lake Museum in Hangzhou also bears the same name, indicating that this individual might either be a Jingdezhen artisan or someone who commissioned the ceramic pieces, making the works extremely rare.

Jierui Tang Collection

Literature: Jeffrey P. Stamen, Cynthia Volk with Yibin Ni, A *Culture Revealed, Kangxi-Era Chinese Porcelain from the Jie Rui Tang Collection,* Bruges, 2017, pl. 30.

醉蓬萊 詠康熙五彩
望月圖詩文筆筒

莘野樵父 升平伊尹
與木石居 與鹿豕遊
妙手運化 摶埴翰墨林
重閣仙榭 天才流麗
追河岳英靈
玉宇無塵 鳳凰鳴吻
案頭瓊筒

王昌齡

聽月樓高太清南山對戶分明

昨夜姮娥現影嫣然笑裡傳聲

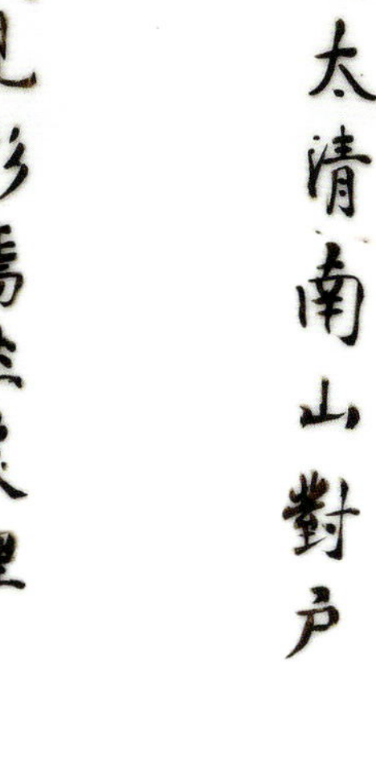

華野樵筆

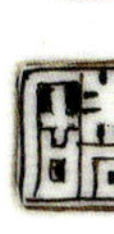

清 康熙

釉里红加五彩花卉纹苹果尊 高：8.5 厘米

大清康熙年制（六字三行楷书款）

陈浏《匋雅》述："苹果尊于苹果绿之外又有天青、釉里红两种，皆珍玩也。"清宫将此类苹果尊命名为"白地红花小口花插"，可见其亦可用于四时插花，作文房花器之用。

是器胎质细腻，釉色莹润，造型小巧，呈苹果形，小口外侈，卷唇，肩腹圆润，上以釉里红加五彩绘花卉纹，每两朵花卉一组，共绘两组，构图巧妙，花朵均以釉里红描绘，发色纯正，枝叶则先以墨彩钩绘脉络再填绿彩。画面简洁，着色淡雅，红花绿叶相互辉映。

康熙苹果尊造型共见三种，一为无胫，口部下凹样式，通体釉里红装饰；一为缩颈样式，见有天蓝釉、豇豆红品种；再者即为若是器之短颈小口，以釉里红加五彩装饰之品种，相似装饰纹样也同样运用于康熙名品马蹄尊。

著录于《求知雅集珍藏中国古陶瓷展》，香港中文大学文物馆，1981 年，图版 144。

QING DYNASTY, KANGXI MARK AND PERIOD

A RARE AND EXCEPTIONAL COPPER-RED AND FAMILLE-VERTE "ROSE" VASE Height: 8.5 cm

It was recorded in Chen Liu's *Tao Ya* (Index of Porcelain): "In addition to apple green, rose vases in azure copper-red are laso exist, which are very precious." The Qing palace named this type of vase a "white-ground, red-floral and small-mouthed vase", signifying its suitability for displaying flowers throughout the seasons as a floral vessel.

This vase is finely potted with a lustrous glaze, showcasing an apple silhouette: a petite stature, small outward-flaring mouth, rolled lip, and a smoothly rounded shoulder and belly. It's adorned with underglaze-red enhanced famille-verte painted floral motifs. It is deliberately painted with a pair of lush flowering rose branches rising from the base. Each flower is outlined in underglaze red, displaying a pure hue, while the leaves are first outlined in black and then filled with green enamel. The overall composition is simple and elegant, with the red flowers and green leaves complementing each other harmoniously. The base is inscribed in underglaze blue with a six-character mark.

During the Kangxi period, apple-form vases were typically of three styles: one with no neck and concave mouth decorated in underglaze-red; one featuring a narrowed neck, observed in sky blue and kidney bean red varieties, and the third, like this piece, featuring a short neck and small mouth, decorated with underglaze-red and famille-verte. Similar decorative patterns can also be seen on renowned Kangxi horseshoe-shaped vases.

Literature: *Exhibition of Ancient Chinese Ceramics: From the Collection of the Kau Chi Society of Chinese Art in Association with the Art Gallery,* the Chinese University of Hong Kong, 1981, pl. 144.

清 康熙

釉里红加五彩花卉纹马蹄尊 直径：13 厘米

大清康熙年制（六字三行楷书款）

是器广口，圆唇，削肩广腹，浅圈足，器形似马蹄状，故名。造型优雅，线条柔美，胎釉细腻肥润，工艺极为精湛。外壁以釉里红及矾红分绘并蒂而生的花卉两株，以绿彩、墨彩加饰枝叶，寥寥数笔，摇曳生姿，尽显清秀。釉里红、五彩交相辉映，别具韵味。画面清寂灵透，秀雅之气跃然而出。

此式马蹄尊有两种构图方式，一式为所绘花卉分两组布局，每组仅以釉里红绘一枝花朵；另一式如是器为一组布局，分别以釉里红与釉上矾红绘制两朵姿态各异且色调不同的红花。是器枝叶先以黑彩排点勾廓，后仅施浓淡不同之绿彩进行描绘。与另一类以褐、绿两色搭配表现枝叶纹理之作品也有不同。

著录于《徐氏艺术馆·瓷器Ⅳ·清代》，徐氏艺术馆，1995 年，图版 122。

QING DYNASTY, KANGXI MARK AND PERIOD

A FINE AND RARE ENAMELLED AND COPPER-RED DECORATED WATER POT, HORSESHOE VASE

Diameter: 13cm

This vessel, shaped like a "Mati" (horseshoe), has a wide mouth, round lip, and a shallow ring foot. The exterior features underglaze red and iron red rendering of two floral sprigs emanating from a common stem, with the foliage further adorned in green and ink tones. The harmonious blend of underglaze and enamels imparts a unique charm, with the painting radiating a serene elegance.

There are two compositional methods for the painting style of such type of horseshoe vase. The first type contains two floral patterns, each of which is of a single underglaze-red flower. The other, like this vessel, features a single group with two distinct blossoms in underglaze red and iron-red glaze. The foliage of this vessel is first outlined with black dots, and then only rendered with varying shades of green, differing from pieces that use both brown and green representing the texture of leaves and branches.

Literature: *The Tsui Museum of Art· Chinese Ceramic IV· Qing Dynasty*, The Tsui Museum of Art, 1995, pl.122.

清 康熙

冬青釉浅浮雕祥云纹马蹄式水盂 高：7.5 厘米

大清康熙年制（六字三行楷书款）

是器形似马蹄，故谓之“马蹄式水盂”，又称“马蹄尊”，为康熙朝盛行之文房用品。外壁以减地起阳纹技法剔刻缕缕祥云，疏朗而飘逸。其釉色莹润，俊雅青翠。器上釉色清澈细润，为宋龙泉青釉之延续。祥云纹始于元代，后续一直沿用，为祥瑞之意。是器简朴俊美，纹饰、工艺精致，盈手可握，形色契合，灵秀巧雅气韵自生。

此式水盂为康熙御窑文房雅具中最典型者，其造型精巧，玲珑可人。《藏盂小志》写道：“试叩问之，若无盂盛以水，岂能染墨濡笔，挥毫于缣素耶？”言其为置于书案上之贮水器，用于贮砚水，为文房一重要器具。

QING DYNASTY, KANGXI MARKED AND PERIOD

A FINE CARVED CELADON-GLAZED “CLOUD” WATER POT

Height: 7.5 cm

This vessel was a prevalent scholar’s article during the Kangxi reign. The outer wall is meticulously carved with flowing auspicious clouds using a raised pattern technique, sparse and elegant. The piece's lustrous celadon glaze, reminiscent of Song Dynasty Longquan celadon, features a continuously used auspicious cloud pattern from the Yuan Dynasty, symbolizing good fortune. The vessel is simple yet elegant, with delicate patterns and craftsmanship, handy and harmonious in shape and color, embodying intrinsic grace and refinement. The base is inscribed Kangxi six- character mark in underglaze blue.

This water pot represents the most typical scholar’s elegant object amongst the imperial kiln of the Kangxi period, with its intricate and pleasing form. It reflects the zenith of artistic achievement and cultural prosperity during the Kangxi period.

清 康熙

青花海水云龙纹文具盒

长：22.9 厘米

此式文具盒源于伊斯兰金属器皿，明永乐朝引入并改以瓷制。

康熙时期瓷制青花文具盒极为罕见。是器盒盖以青花绘制海水云龙纹，边饰一周青花回纹。盒身外壁以青花绘蟠螭纹，同北京故宫博物院清宫旧藏康熙青花蟠螭纹缸纹饰相近，盒内亦分成一个承水格与三个调色格。全器工艺考究，制作复杂，青花发色鲜艳。

洁蕊堂旧藏

著录于 R.L. 霍布森：《乔治·欧莫夫普洛斯 珍藏中国、朝鲜及波斯陶器》，第五册，伦敦，1926 年，图版 5，编号 E.34；杰弗里·施塔门，辛西娅·沃尔克，倪亦斌编：《文采卓然：洁蕊堂藏康熙盛世瓷》，布鲁日，2017 年，图版 24。

QING DYNASTY, KANGXI PERIOD

A RARE BLUE AND WHITE "DRAGON" CALLIGRAPHY BOX WITH COVER

Length: 22.9 cm

This type of calligraphy box is sourced from Islamic metalwork and was introduced into China during the Yongle era of the Ming Dynasty, subsequently adapted and recreated in porcelain.

The blue and white porcelain calligraphy box from the Kangxi period are exceedingly rare. The lid is painted with a sinuous, writhing dragon emerging from roiling and cresting waves with scudding skies overhead, encircled by a leiwen border. The exterior wall of the box is painted with a panchi pattern, akin to the design found on a Kangxi blue and white panchi pattern tank stored in the Palace Museum, Beijing, previously a part of the Qing palace collection. The interior of the box is also segmented into one water-holding compartment and three ink-mixing compartments. The overall craft of this piece is meticulous, with a complex production process.

Jierui Tang Collection

Literature: R. L. HOBSON, *The Catalogue of the George Eumorfopoulos Collection of Chinese, Corean and Persian Pottery and Porcelain,* Vol.V, London, 1926, pl.5, lot. E34. Jeffrey P. Stamen, Cynthia Volk with Yibin Ni, *A Culture Revealed, Kangxi-Era Chinese Porcelain from the Jie Rui Tang Collection,* Bruges, 2017, pl. 24.

清 康熙

青花五彩八月桂花花神杯

直径：6.2 厘米

大清康熙年制（六字双行楷书款）

题识：枝生无限月，花满自然秋　钤印：赏

此杯为十二月令花神杯之“八月桂花”。《匋雅》述此式八月花神杯“彩花以有黄色小兔者为最美”。考十二月令花神杯之实况，其烧造时间共两次，前一次为康熙十九年至二十七年间（1680—1688），写款为楷书两行竖款；后一次为康熙晚期，写款为宋椠体三行横款。

是器形制小巧，口沿微撇，深腹，上腹斜直，下腹微收，底承圈足。胎釉莹润似玉，质薄如纸，设色雅丽。外壁以青花五彩绘十二花神之《八月桂花图》，一树桂花绽放枝头，树下玉兔回首眺望，灵动可人，并题唐人佳句“枝生无限月，花满自然秋”，末钤“赏”字篆文印。

枝生無限月
花滿自然秋

QING DYNASTY, KANGXI MARK AND PERIOD

A WUCAI “OSMANTHUS” MONTHLY CUP

Diameter: 6.2cm

This cup, adorned with osmanthus motifs, signifies August in the series representing the twelve months, correlating with the time when osmanthus bloom. This period coincides with the Mid-Autumn Festival, traditionally celebrated on the 15th day of the eighth lunar month.The vessel is delicately crafted with a slightly flared lip, deep belly, straight upper belly, slightly tapered lower belly, and a ring-footed base. The glaze is luminous, reminiscent of jade, and thin as paper, with elegant colors. The outer wall is adorned with blue and white wucai depicting the osmanthus, where an osmanthus tree in full bloom extends its branches and beneath which a graceful and endearing hare looks up to the moon. The reverse inscribed in underglaze blue with a poem and concluded with a with a mark of shang (appreciation).

清 康熙

青花五彩六月荷花花神杯 直径：6.2 厘米

大清康熙年制（六字双行楷书款）

题识：根是泥中玉，心承露下珠　钤印：赏

十二月令花神杯为康熙御窑之名品，按图与诗意，此杯为十二月令花神杯之“六月荷花”，较之其他月令杯，此六月杯存世极为少见。

是器胎薄如纸，造型秀巧玲珑，白釉莹润。器身外壁以五彩装饰六月花神荷花图，荷花于仲夏时节开放，于碧水间亭亭玉立，清新淡雅，芳华内蕴，超逸脱俗。一侧题写唐李群玉诗句“根是泥中玉，心承露下珠”，末钤“赏”字印。

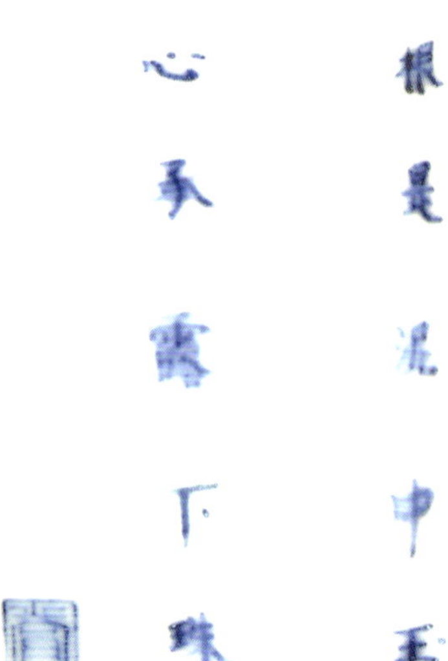

QING DYNASTY, KANGXI MARK AND PERIOD

A RARE WUCAI "LOTUS" MONTHLY CUP Diameter: 6.2cm

Month cups depicting seasonal flowers were renowned products of the Kangxi imperial kilns. Compared to other monthly cups, this June version is extremely rare.

The vessel is thinly potted, almost paper-thin, with an exquisite and delicate design. The glaze is luminous and smooth. The external wall of the vessel is adorned with the colorful image of lotus. The lotus, which blossoms in mid-summer, stands elegantly amidst clear waters, exuding a fresh and refined beauty, its charm subtle yet profound, transcending the mundane. The reverse inscribed in underglaze blue with a poem followed by a seal mark reading shang (appreciation).

The poem can be translated as follows: "The roots are like jade gleaming in the mud. The hearts contain pearls when dew has descended."

清 康熙

珊瑚红地瓷胎画珐琅九秋图宫碗

直径：11厘米

康熙御制（四字双行楷书款）

是器外壁于珊瑚红地上以黑彩勾勒九秋图轮廓，内填红、蓝、绿、紫等诸色，通过色彩浓淡变化来表现花叶之阴阳向背。整器色彩缤纷，绘画精湛，布局繁密而有致，益见设计构图之佳妙。因秋天乃收获季节，遂汇集九种秋草于一图，寓意九秋同庆，共贺丰收。底青花双框内楷书"康熙御制"，极为可贵。此"康熙御制"四字款，为内府标准之书体，笔道硬朗，端庄周正，青花深沉，紧贴胎骨，为康熙御瓷标准款式。

"御制"款较之"年制"款者，更为稀少，亦彰显与皇室更密切的关系。五彩御瓷中未见署写"康熙御制"之款式，唯独珐琅彩瓷方见。是器之彩釉画法与康熙朝珐琅彩瓷毫无差别，尤其写款一项，当属康熙朝珐琅彩瓷之品类。

QING DYNASTY, KANGXI MARK AND PERIOD

A FINE AND RARE CORAL-GROUND FAMILLE-VERTE FLORAL BOWL

Diameter: 11 cm

The exterior of this bowl showcases nine autumnal plants outlined on a coral red ground with black enameling, filled with vibrant colors of red, blue, green, and purple. The color intensity skillfully illustrates the light and shadow on the foliage. The piece displays a rich color palette, exquisite painting, and a well-arranged layout, reflecting a remarkable design themed around autumn's harvest. Nine varieties of autumnal plants symbolize a collective celebration of abundant harvest through nine autumns. The base bears the prized four-character mark "Kangxi Yu Zhi" (Kangxi Imperially Made) in underglaze blue within a double square.

The mark yuzhi (imperially made) signifies a closer royal association compared to the mark nianzhi (year made), and is rarely found in famille-verte imperial ware. Only enamel-colored pieces bear the mark Kangxi Yuzhi (imperially made in Kangxi era). The enameling and color palette of this bowl align with the Kangxi period enamel-colored porcelain, notably the inscription style, marking it a distinguished category within this period's enamel-colored porcelain.

清 康熙

青花斗绿彩赶珠云龙纹大盘

直径：25 厘米

大清康熙年制（六字双行楷书款）

绿彩云龙纹盘始见于明代成化时期，为明清两代御窑的经典品种。是器为清初御窑厂建立后，通过以明代绿龙盘为模板所诞出之首代具有清代特色的绿彩龙纹盘。

是器纹饰繁满，画工精细，线条流畅。盘外壁以青花斗绿彩绘火焰腾龙纹与十字祥云纹，烈焰翻滚间，腾龙奔驰有力，盘心所绘龙纹威严，龙身呈“弓”形，身姿矫健，眼神犀利如锋，形态凶猛。其装饰方法系在成型胎上先用青花勾勒纹样的轮廓线后填色，形成斗彩绿龙的色泽效果。绿彩鲜艳明亮，青花浓淡不一。康熙一朝此类单色斗彩瓷器传世数量远不及雍、乾时期多，所见完美者极少，十分珍贵。

著录于《香港苏富比二十周年》1973—1993 年，香港，1993 年，图版 378。

QING DYNASTY, KANGXI MARK AND PERIOD

A FINE AND RARE GREEN-ENAMELLED “DRAGON” DISH

Diameter: 25 cm

The green-enamelled dragon motif dish originated in the Chenghua era of the Ming Dynasty, becoming a classic in the imperial kilns across the Ming and Qing Dynasties. This dish, embodying distinct Qing Dynasty traits, emerged as a first-generation green-enamelled dragon motif dish post the establishment of the imperial kiln factories in early Qing, drawing inspiration from the Ming era's prototype.

The dish, with its meticulous craftsmanship, displays a vibrant dragon motif amidst flames and auspicious clouds, using blue and green enamels. The exterior portrays two fiery dragons in robust vigour, while the center features a majestic dragon with a “bow” shaped body, graceful posture, and a fierce demeanor. The decorative technique starts with blue enamels outlining the design, then colors are filled in, creating a doucai effect. The green enamel is vibrant, and the blue varies in intensity. Fewer monochrome doucai pieces from the Kangxi era survived compared to the Yongzheng and Qianlong periods, making the perfect examples extremely precious.

Literature: *Sotheby's Hong Kong twenty years: 1973-1993,* Hong Kong, 1993, pl. 378.

義正閣

YIZHENG GE PORCELAIN ALBUM

清 雍正

QING DYNASTY, YONGZHENG PERIOD

清 雍正

斗彩鸡缸杯

直径：8.2 厘米

大清雍正年制（六字双行楷书款）

是器承袭15世纪明成化名器之形，然绘画构图破旧立新，以意创造，精工秀丽。对比成化鸡缸杯例，饶有趣味。参考仇焱之旧藏或玫茵堂旧藏成化鸡缸杯，曾为利奥波德·德雷福斯夫人宝蓄，纵然悉绘子母鸡图，画公鸡偕母率幼雏觅食，园中且有花叶秀石，但雍正杯上雄鸡位置有别，尾毛蓬松而非如成化典型分成三簇，黄彩萱草丛改画竹，伴以萱花一朵，另一面月桂秀石之布局也异于前。

仇焱之藏成化例，图刊于西塞尔和米歇尔·贝鲁德利编《中国陶瓷》，同书并录仇氏藏康熙、雍正款例，但其清朝例子，临摹成窑鸡缸细致逼真，沿袭昔时器形、画风、布局、双方框款，有别于此杯处，便是公鸡尾巴也同饰羽毛三簇。

虽宋人早将“子母鸡图”入画，但是成化朝才始饰瓷上。雍正年间，窑烧技术发展至顶峰，并研发出彩釉新品种，特别是以带有光泽的墨彩，描绘鸡尾，与其它釉彩产生鲜明的对比，令纹饰更为生动逼真。成化斗彩设色虽多，但不用墨彩，只在钴蓝上加添绿彩，以达墨色之效。而康熙黑彩呈色缺乏稳定性，须再上浅绿或紫彩以达效果。

此雍正鸡缸杯同类之品，忠于成化器形，然画风更细腻，公鸡尾部高翘，八只小鸡分散而行，花草秀石布局比例也异于成化雏型。

著录于《香港苏富比三十周年》，香港，2003年，图版184。朱汤生：《中国瓷器：庄绍绥收藏》，香港，2009年，图版52。

QING DYNASTY, YONGZHENG MARK AND PERIOD

A RARE DOUCAI CHICKEN CUP

Diameter: 8.2 cm

This vessel inherits the form of renowned 15th-century Chenghua ceramics from the Ming Dynasty, yet innovates with a fresh illustration composition, skillfully and exquisitely crafted. When juxtaposed with the Chenghua chicken cup, the comparison is intriguing. Referring to collections of Edward T. Chow or the Meiyintang Collection, once treasured by Madame Leopold Dreyfus, both depict a hen and rooster leading chicks to forage in a garden adorned with flowers, leaves, and rocks. However, the position of the rooster on the Yongzheng cup diverges; its tail feathers are depicted as loose rather than the typical three-cluster formation seen in Chenghua's era. The yellow daylily bushes are reimagined as bamboo, accompanied by a single daylily flower, with the layout of the flowers and rocks on the other side also differing from its predecessor.

The Chenghua example from Edward T. Chow's collection, illustrated in Cécile et Michel Beurdeley's *La Céramique Chinoise,* alongside other Kangxi and Yongzheng examples from Chow's collection, demonstrates Qing Dynasty pieces meticulously emulating Chenghua kiln's chicken cups in terms of vessel shape, artistic style, composition, and double square framing. Unlike this cup, those examples also maintained the three-cluster feather decoration on the rooster's tail.

The "Rooster and chicks" motif started adorning ceramics during the Chenghua era. By the Yongzheng era, advancements in kiln technologies had reached their zenith, resulting in a creation of new varieties of colored glazes. Among these was the lustrous ink glaze, which was notably used to outline rooster tails, providing a vibrant contrast with other glazes and lending the designs a lively and realistic quality. Chenghua doucai ceramics were known for their use of multiple hues but did not incorporate this ink glaze. Instead, artisans achieved a black effect by layering green over cobalt blue. Kangxi black color lacked stability, necessitating an additional overlay of light green or purple to achieve the desired effect.

This Yongzheng chicken cup, while faithful to the Chenghua vessel shape, exhibits a more delicate painting style.

Literature: *Sotheby's thirty years in Hong Kong,* Hong Kong, 2003, pl.184.

Julian Thompson, *The Alan Chuang Collection of Chinese Porcelain,* Hong Kong, 2009, pl. 61.

清 雍正

斗彩团菊纹杯 直径：7.3 厘米

大清雍正年制（六字双行楷书款）

此式团菊小杯为雍正御窑追慕成窑作品而成。唐英《陶成纪事碑记》称之为"仿成化窑淡描青花"。此式团菊纹样在雍、乾之时见有杯、碗、罐等多种造型，并有斗彩及青花淡描品种。

是器敞口，深腹，下承圈足，胎体轻薄，胎质细腻洁白，修足规整。腹部以斗彩绘团簇菊纹，其间以卷草花卉纹分隔。花叶勾勒细腻，填彩准确，绘工精湛，体现雍正御窑器制作之精细，具有鲜丽清逸之气。

著录于马钱特：《清瓷》，伦敦，2011 年，图版 27。

QING DYNASTY, YONGZHENG MARK AND PERIOD

A FINE DOUCAI "CHRYSANTHEMUM MEDALLION" WINE CUP

Diameter: 7.3 cm

This chrysanthemum medallion cup originates from the Yongzheng Imperial kiln, embodying the admiration for the Chenghua kiln works. The chrysanthemum motif was adapted into various forms like cups, bowls, and jars during the Yongzheng and Qianlong periods, available both in doucai and light blue-and-white sketch versions.

The cup, with its open mouth and deep belly, stands on a ring foot. Its body is light and thin, crafted from clay that is finely delicate and pristine. The belly is adorned with doucai motifs of clustered chrysanthemums, interspersed with scrolling foliage. The delicate outlining of the flower petals and the precision in color filling demonstrate exquisite craftsmanship, embodying the finesse of Yongzheng Imperial kiln wares and exuding an aura of fresh elegance. The base inside the double square ring is inscribed in underglaze blue with the Yongzheng six-character mark.

Literature: Marchant, *Qing Porcelain,* London, 2011, cat. no 27.

清 雍正

斗彩暗八仙纹碗 直径：13.2 厘米

大清雍正年制（六字双行楷书款）

暗八仙为瓷器传统纹饰，以八仙手中执物暗喻代指，寓意祝颂长寿。仅择神仙所执，不现仙人，为中国艺术表现中具有悠久传统的暗喻手法。

是器敞口，弧腹，圈足。外壁近口沿处饰绶带纹，碗身绘暗八仙，下部饰如意云纹。内壁口部饰青花双圈弦纹，底部双圈内饰双桃淡雅清丽，寓意八仙贺寿，为清宫祝寿时用器。整器绘制细腻精湛，布局合理，繁而不乱。青花幽亮静恬，红彩纯正匀净，绿彩娇嫩青翠，黄彩明快润泽，诸色相配，殊得趣韵。

QING DYNASTY, YONGZHENG MARK AND PERIOD

A FINE DOUCAI "ANBAXIAN" BOWL Diameter: 13.2 cm

The Anbaxian motif, or "Hidden Eight Immortals", is a traditional design in Chinese porcelain, symbolizing longevity through the items held by the Eight Immortals without depicting their figures. It reflects a rich tradition of metaphorical expression in Chinese artistry.

The vessel features a wide mouth with a curved belly and a circled foot. Near the rim of the exterior, a ribbon pattern is adorned, with the body of the bowl illustrating the Anbaxian, and the lower portion embellished with auspicious cloud motifs. The inner rim showcases a blue-and-white double-circle string pattern, while within the double circles at the base, a delicate and elegant depiction of twin peaches is presented, symbolizing the Eight Immortals conveying blessings for longevity, a type of vessel used for celebrating longevity in the Qing Imperial court. The piece boasts remarkable meticulous painting and a rational layout with intricate yet organized detailing. The harmonious blend of tranquil blue-and-white, pure red, tender green, and bright yellow colors enhances its aesthetic appeal.

清 雍正

矾红夔凤纹水盂 直径：5.7 厘米

大清雍正年制（六字双行楷书款）

是器圆口微撇，短束颈部，深弧腹，圈足。外壁颈部、下腹饰变形蚕纹各一周，腹部以矾红描绘夔凤纹。所绘夔凤鹰嘴利爪，翎羽飞扬，绘画技法以平涂及留白为主，仅以深浅不同的两种红色表现。此器制作严谨，胎釉精良，风格奇诡，为雍正御窑文房稀见品种。

器中所绘夔凤纹，乃据夔龙纹创造之凤纹，古朴简练，在西周青铜器上即已出现，象征尊贵身份。是器纹饰即对古代器皿崇以至高敬意，为雍正御窑文房稀见品种。

仇炎之旧藏

QING DYNASTY, YONGZHENG MARK AND PERIOD

A RARE IRON-RED DECORATED PHOENIX WATERPOT

Height: 5.7 cm

This artifact has a round mouth with a slight flare, a short bundled neck, a deep arc belly, and a ring foot. The exterior neck and lower belly are adorned with a transformed silkworm pattern circling around, while the belly section is depicted with an iron-red phoenix pattern. The depicted phoenix has a hawk beak and sharp claws. The painting technique primarily employs flat coloring and white spacing, utilizing only two shades of red to illustrate varying depths. The rigor in craftsmanship, superior glaze quality, and peculiar style make this piece a rare find among the imperial kiln scholar objects from the Yongzheng period. The base is inscribed with "Da Qing Yongzheng Nian Zhi" (Made in the Yongzheng era of the Great Qing) in regular script, in underglaze blue. The phoenix pattern drawn on this vessel is derived from the ancient Kui dragon pattern, simplified yet quaint. This pattern, already appearing on Western Zhou dynasty bronzeware, symbolizes a noble status. The pattern on this artifact reflects a high regard for ancient vessels, making it a rare specimen among the imperial kiln scholar objects of the contemporary court.

Collection of Edward T. Chow

清 雍正

柠檬黄釉茶圆一对 直径：9.4 厘米 ×2

大清雍正年制（六字双行楷书款）

柠檬黄釉为清唐英督窑期间所创烧之黄釉新品，因色如柠檬，故称柠檬黄釉。清代文献亦称之为“西洋黄”“洋黄”。

是器斜直壁，阔圈足，倒置形如马蹄，故亦有“马蹄杯”之称。此式杯形出现于康熙晚期，雍正时期沿袭烧制此造型作品。是器造型秀巧，内壁施白釉，外壁施柠檬黄釉，纯净娇嫩，明丽夺目，搭配轻盈灵透的器形，形色相配，相得益彰。检索公私收藏，此式马蹄造型的柠檬黄釉作品仅见此一对，甚为珍罕。

天民楼旧藏

著录及展览：香港艺术馆、香港市政局，《天民楼藏瓷（上册）》，中华商务联合印刷（香港）有限公司，1987 年，图版 139。《众彩煌煌 —— 敏求精舍中国瓷器装饰艺术解读》，华盛顿赛克勒美术馆，1993 年，第 75 页，图版 4。

QING DYNASTY, YONGZHENG MARK AND PERIOD

A PAIR OF VERY RARE YELLOW GLAZE BOWLS Diameter: 9.4cm×2

The lemon-yellow glaze is a new type of yellow glaze created during the Yongzheng period when Tang Ying served as the official superintendent of porcelain. Named for its lemon-like hue, this glaze is also referred to as “Western Yellow” or “Foreign Yellow” in Qing dynasty documents.

This pair features a sloped straight wall design and a broad-rimmed foot, resembling an inverted horseshoe when turned upside down, hence they are also known as “Horseshoe Cups”. This style emerged during the late Kangxi period and continued to be crafted during the Yongzheng era. The design of these vessels is elegant, lightweight, and translucent. The inner wall is coated with a white glaze, while the outer wall is adorned with the lemon yellow glaze, emanating purity, delicacy, and a bright, eye-catching appearance. This harmonizes well with the lightweight and translucent form of the vessels, enhancing each other's beauty. The base is inscribed in underglaze blue with the mark “Da Qing Yongzheng Nian Zhi” (Made during the Qing Yongzheng era of the Great Qing) in regular script. Upon investigation of both public and private collections, this particular pair with a horseshoe design in lemon yellow glaze is the only one of its kind rendering it exceptionally rare.

Tianminlou Collection

Literature: *Chinese Porcelain. The S.C. Ko Tianminlou Collection,* Vol. 1, Hong Kong: Hong Kong Museum Of Art, 1987, pl. 139. *Joined Colors—Decoration and Meaning in Chinese Porcelain: Ceramics from Collectors in the Mingqiu Society,* Hong Kong, Arthur M. Sackler Gallery, 1993, p. 75, pl.4.

清 雍正

松石绿釉葵式茶碗一对 直径：11.5 厘米 ×2

大清雍正年制（六字双行楷书款）

松石绿釉为雍正御窑新创，呈色淡绿至深绿不等，色深者似绿松石色泽，故以“松石绿”命名，为宫廷用器中之尊贵色釉。

是器状若盛开之葵花，口呈八朵花瓣状，亦为点睛。婉转圆润，体线推敲琢磨，无可增减。外壁通体施松石绿釉，釉色匀柔，莹润如玉。松石绿釉多为彩瓷色地，以彰彩绘之美，而此式工艺不独如此，更多突出松石绿釉之匀净质感及器物形体之美。

展览：美国得克萨斯州圣安东尼奥美术馆（1984—2017）。

QING DYNASTY, YONGZHENG MARK AND PERIOD

A VERY RARE PAIR OF MOULDED TURQUOISE-ENAMELLED MALLOW-FORM TEA BOWLS

Diameter: 11.5cm×2

The turquoise glaze was in novatively crafted in the imperial kilns during Yongzheng's reign, exhibiting a color range from light to deep green. The deeper shade resembles the color and texture of green turquoise, giving the glaze its name and distinguished status among courtly tableware.

Each bowl is delicately moulded with a band of petal lappets above the foot rim, below swirling and overlapping mallow-flower petals flaring to corresponding lobed rim, serving as a charming highlight. The outer surface is entirely covered with an opaque turquoise enamel stopping neatly around the foot rim, presenting a soft, even, and jade-like lustrous finish. While turquoise glaze is often used as the colored ground for polychrome porcelains to accentuate the beauty of colorful paintings, this particular craftsmanship transcends that tradition, emphasizing the pure and uniform texture of the turquoise glaze and the aesthetic form of the object.

Exhibited: San Antonio Museum of Art, Texas, USA, 1984-2017.

清 雍正

霁红釉小瓶 高：12.1 厘米

大清雍正年制（六字双行楷书款）

清代霁红釉仿明代永宣红釉而烧造，雍正时期多见盘、碗及玉壶春瓶等造型，器形独特的赏玩小器极少。

是器尺寸小巧，可执于掌中把玩。撇口，圆唇，束颈，溜肩，束腹，器形挺拔俊秀，线条柔美起伏，通体施霁红釉，红釉色泽鲜艳夺目，通体颜色一致，极为难得。瓶里及足底均施白釉，是器造型线条优美流畅，器小体轻，亦为一例文房雅品。

著录于朱汤生：《中国瓷器：庄绍绥收藏》，香港，2009 年，图版 63。

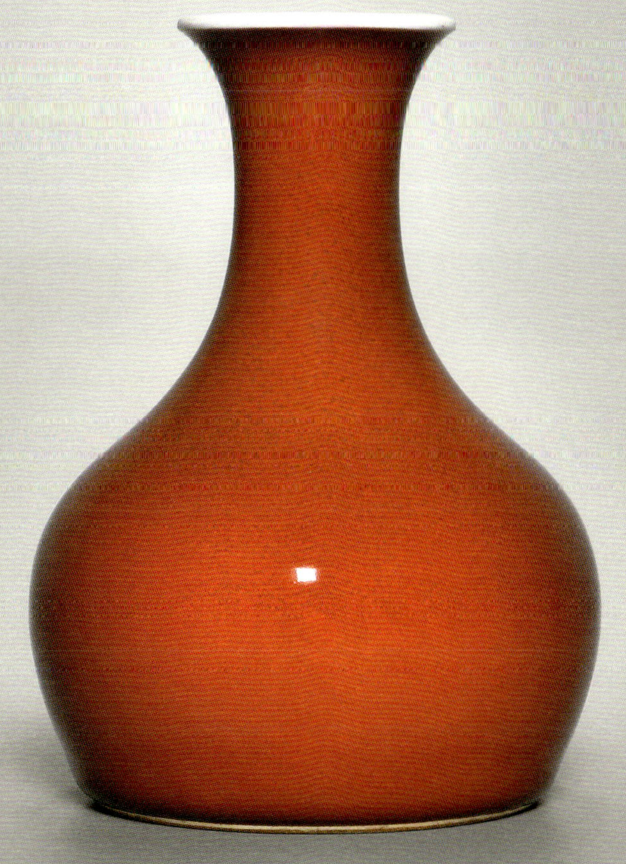

QING DYNASTY, YONGZHENG MARK AND PERIOD

A RARE COPPER-RED GLAZED VASE

Height: 12.1cm

During the Qing Dynasty, Ji Hong glaze (copper red) was crafted to imitate the Ming Dynasty's Yongle and Xuande red glaze, with the Yongzheng period often showcasing plates, bowls, and YuHuchun vases. However, small ornamental pieces with unique shapes were rare.

This piece is compact in size, making it a delightful handheld artifact for appreciation. It features a flaring mouth, round lip, constrained neck, smooth shoulders, and a tight belly, which together contribute to its upright and graceful form. The gentle and flowing lines exhibit a soft aesthetic. The vase is entirely coated with Ji Hong glaze, whose bright red hue is striking and captivating. The uniform color throughout the body of the vase makes it extremely precious. Both the interior and the foot of the vase are coated with white glaze, with a blue-and-white inscription on the base reading "Da Qing Yongzheng Nian Zhi" (Made during the Yongzheng era of the Great Qing) in regular script. The elegant and fluid form, light weight, and small size make this vase a refined piece of scholar's paraphernalia.

Literature: Julian Thompson, *The Alan Chuang Collection of Chinese Porcelain*, Hong Kong, 2009, pl. 63.

清 雍正

霁蓝釉胆瓶一对

高：19.5 厘米 ×2

大清雍正年制（六字双行楷书款）

蓝釉始于元代，为明清官窑的重要品种，清代御窑将此釉色专称为"霁青"，取光风霁月、澄雅宜人之意。

胆瓶因形如悬胆而得名，宋代已烧造，最宜插花。是器直口长颈，削肩鼓腹，敛归圆底，承以圈足。体线优化，凝练合度，盈手可握，精雅之至。瓶外壁满施霁釉，釉色如蓝宝石般晶莹剔透，纯净宁谧。成对传世，更显珍贵。全器风格幽隽凝素而工艺极精，展现出雍正御瓷清雅含蓄之风。

QING DYNASTY, YONGZHENG MARK AND PERIOD

A PAIR OF VERY RARE BOTTLE VASES WITH BLUE GLAZE

Height: 19.5 cm×2

The tradition of blue glaze began in the Yuan Dynasty and was a significant category of the official kilns during the Ming and Qing dynasties. In the Qing imperial kiln, this glaze color, cobalt blue was specifically referred to as "Ji Qing", symbolizing clear and pleasant weather, embodying an air of refined elegance. The name "Dan bottle" (bottle vase) is derived from its gallbladder-like shape, with its origins tracing back to the Song Dynasty, making it a suitable vessel for flower arrangement. The vase features a straight mouth, a long neck, sloped shoulders, a round belly, tapering down to a round base, standing on a ring foot. The contours are optimized to a refined and well-proportioned design, comfortable to hold, epitomizing elegance. The exterior of the vase is fully coated with Ji Qing glaze, rendering a luster akin to sapphire, pure and serene. The vases come in a pair, enhancing their preciousness. The entire piece exudes a graceful and exquisite charm, showcasing the refined and understated elegance of Yongzheng imperial porcelain.

清 雍正

斗彩缠枝西番莲纹长颈瓶 高 24.5 厘米

大清雍正年制（六字双行楷书款）

是器盘口，长颈，渐转溜肩，垂扁鼓腹，圈足。周身光素，纯以形优，营造出稳固和谐之均势。通体绘斗彩纹样，以青花弦线作边饰，外壁绘缠枝西番莲纹，枝蔓繁茂蜿蜒，清新素雅。花瓣以诸色绘就，各尽其妍。足墙饰卷草纹，勾画婉转流畅。纹饰布局清新疏朗，填色精准，釉彩娇嫩润泽，为雍正仿成化瓷器中珍罕之作品。仅西藏博物馆存有与是器造型纹饰相同之藏品。是器足部造型虽带清朝特色，但观其器形整体却是明成化风格，传世品中极为罕见。

大清雍正年製

QING DYNASTY, YONGZHENG MARK AND PERIOD

A VERY RARE DOUCAI VASE WITH ENTWINED BRANCHES AND LOTUS DESIGN Height: 24.5 cm

This exquisite vase boasts a flared rim, elongated neck, gradually transitioning to sloping shoulders, flat and round belly, leading to a circular foot. Its smooth, undecorated surface celebrates the vessel's elegant form, contributing to a harmonious and stable aesthetic. The vase's exterior is adorned with intricate doucai motifs, bordered by blue-and-white string patterns. Its body features entwined branch lotus patterns, with flourishing, meandering vines exuding a fresh and refined elegance. The lotus petals are meticulously painted in various colors, each showcasing its beauty. The base wall is decorated with scroll grass patterns, presenting a fluid and graceful outline. The arrangement of the decorative elements is fresh and open, with precise color filling and a delicate, moist glaze. Inscribed on the base in blue is the phrase “Da Qing Yongzheng Nian Zhi” (Made in the Yongzheng era of the Great Qing) in regular script, signifying this vase as a rare work of Yongzheng's imitation of Chenghua porcelain. It's found that only the Tibet Museum holds a piece in similar form and decoration. While the foot's shape bears characteristics of the Qing Dynasty, the overall form of the vase resonates with the style of Chenghua era in the Ming Dynasty, making it an extremely rare item among existing pieces.

燕歸梁

詠雍正斗彩纏枝西番蓮紋長頸瓶

香草搖然花纏枝
彩蓮萬斛
腰肢裊裊影婆娑
霜月銀燈星漢下
瓶中花羞繚繞

清 雍正

窑变釉双耳盘口瓶 高：35 厘米

雍正年制（四字双行篆书款）

是器洗口长颈，方折肩，腹部下敛，圈足外侈；颈部饰双耳，肩部及胫部各饰模印如意云纹一周，并缀弦纹两道。口沿、双耳及如意云纹浅露白筋，呈现静谧润洁的月白之色。通体施窑变釉，釉面莹润光洁，铜红釉自上而下自然流淌，宛若瀑布泻流而下。足内施釉斑驳自然。

是器之如意云肩尤为别致，或烧制于雍正末期，并延续至乾隆早期。乾隆二年（1737）十月十三日之《各作成做活计清档》载“唐英所进瓷器内……均釉拱如意花瓶……不必烧造”，或指此类器，可见其烧制时间极短，故存世量极少。是器造型独特，极为少见。

怀海堂旧藏

著录于《机暇清赏：怀海堂藏清代御窑瓷瓶》，香港中文大学出版社，2007 年，页 220—221，编号 67。

展览：香港中文大学文物馆，“机暇清赏 —— 怀海堂藏清代御窑瓷瓶”，2007 年 11 月 11 日至 2008 年 3 月 30 日。

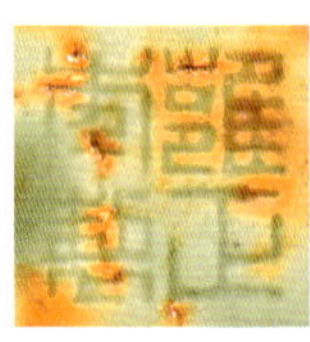

QING DYNASTY, YONGZHENG MARK AND PERIOD

A VERY RARE VASE WITH FLAMBÉ GLAZE Height: 35 cm

This vessel exhibits a long neck with square-folded shoulders, constricted lower belly, and out-turned ring foot. The neck is adorned with double ears, with the shoulder and lower body section are each decorated with a round of mold-impressed ruyi cloud motifs, further embellished with two corded bands. The rim and double handles of the piece, adorned with ruyi cloud motifs, subtly reveal streaks of white, gives it a tranquil and lustrous moon-white appearance. The entire body is covered with a flambé glaze, which is glossy and smooth. The copper-red glaze naturally flows downward from top, resembling a waterfall cascading down. The interior of the foot exhibits a natural, mottled glaze, beneath which is incised a seal mark of Yongzheng Nian Zhi (Made during the reign of Yongzheng).

The ruyi cloud shoulders of this vessel are notably unique, possibly crafted during the late Yongzheng era and extended into the early Qianlong period. As recorded in Various Craftsmanship Production Records on the 13th day of lunar October 1737, "Among the porcelain pieces presented by Tang Ying… the evenly glazed ruyi flower vase…needs not to be fired." possibly referring to this type of vessel, indicating a very short production period, hence very few have survived. This vessel possesses a unique shape, extremely rare.

The Huaihaitang Collection

Literature: *Ethereal Elegance: Porcelain Vases of the Imperial Qing-The Huaihaitang Collection*, the Chinese univerrsity of Hong Kong Press, 2007.

清 雍正

洒蓝地白花缠枝花卉纹盘

直径：33.2 厘米

大清雍正年制（六字双行楷书款）

洒蓝釉又名“雪花蓝釉”，吹釉于器上，故又称“吹青”，创烧于明代宣德时期，康熙时期已臻成熟，雍正时期在洒蓝釉上添加堆白工艺。

是器体量颇大，敞口弧壁，底承矮圈足。盘内外壁均以洒蓝釉为底色，其上以堆白之手法装饰栀子花纹样，花卉蓝白相间，色泽对比分外醒目，纹样工整而雅致。底青花书“大清雍正年制”楷书款，字迹规整，笔画有力。此类洒蓝釉堆白作品，制作工序复杂，先于素坯之上依图堆塑出缠枝花卉纹饰并覆上白釉，入窑素烧成为瓷胎，继而于素胎之处施蓝釉二度入窑，方始完成。

QING DYNASTY, YONGZHENG MARK AND PERIOD

A RARE REVERSE-DECORATED POWDER-BLUE “GARDENIA” DISH

Diameter: 33.2 cm

The technique of “Blue-Splashed Glaze”, involves blowing glaze onto the ceramic piece, hence it's also referred to as “Chui qing”. This technique was first fired during the Xuande period of the Ming dynasty, matured by the Kangxi era, and was further refined during the Yongzheng era with the addition of piled-white craftsmanship. This particular piece is of significant size, with an open mouth and curved walls, resting on a low ring foot. Both the inner and outer walls are coated with splashed-blue glaze as the base color, adorned with white-piled gardenia patterns. The juxtaposition of blue and white floral designs offers a distinctive contrast, making the details exceptionally eye-catching, with a neat and elegant pattern work. The bottom features the inscription “Da Qing Yongzheng Nian Zhi” (Made during the Yongzheng era of the Great Qing) in regular script, with well-structured characters and firm strokes. The creation of such splashed-blue with piled-white artworks involves a complex process. Initially, the twined branch floral decorations are molded onto the blank body, coated with white glaze, and fired in the kiln to form a porcelain body. Following this, blue glaze is applied to the porcelain body, and it's re-entered into the kiln for a second firing, marking the successful completion of the piece.

清 雍正

青花加矾红折枝宝相花纹杯 直径：8.1 厘米

大清雍正年制（六字双行楷书款）

是器撇口，弧腹，浅圈足，形制规整，胎壁盈薄。外壁以矾红绘宝相花纹四朵，以青花平涂枝叶，又称“地涌金莲”纹。胎质细腻洁白，釉面光洁莹润，一如成窑之柔美，矾红彩细润明艳，青花发色纯正，对比强烈，呼之欲出，更显妍丽。款识亦沿袭成化朝样式，于双方框内以青花书“大清雍正年制”楷书款，字体秀雅。此式品种之烧造，始于明成化官窑，系参照红蓝宝石镶嵌器皿而制。

QING DYNASTY, YONGZHENG MARK AND PERIOD

A FINE UNDERGLAZE-BLUE AND IRON-RED "LOTUS" CUP Diameter: 8.1 cm

This cup features a flared mouth, rounded belly, and shallow ring foot, embodying a well-proportioned and meticulously crafted form. The outer surface is adorned with four treasure flower motifs painted in iron-red, complemented by underglaze blue for the foliage that is also referred to as the 'golden lotus' pattern. The body of the porcelain is finely textured and pure white, with a glaze that is smooth, bright, and reminiscent of the soft beauty from the Chenghua kiln. The iron-red color is finely and brightly rendered, while the underglaze blue presents a pure hue. Such strong contrast between the two makes the design vivid and lively, further accentuating the cup's elegance. The mark follows the tradition of the Chenghua era, with the six-character reign mark of "Da Qing Yongle Nian Zhi" (Made during the Yongzheng era of the Great Qing) written in underglaze blue regular script within a double square frame on the base. The creation of this style began with the the Chenghua official kiln of the Ming Dynasty, inspired by the design of red and blue gem-inlaid vessels.

清 雍正

斗彩菊花捧寿纹盘 直径：20 厘米

大清雍正年制（六字双行楷书款）

是器盘心绘丛菊捧寿纹，外壁绘六组折枝丛菊，间以勾连纹；相似纹饰者尚见有碗、梅瓶、如意耳蒜头瓶等器型，均为雍正时期作品。纹饰填彩精确，布局繁密，以多层彩料渲染菊花，叶片卷曲具西洋装饰风格，阴阳向背，质感逼真。底青花书“大清雍正年制”楷书款。盘内外所绘丛菊，由雏菊和石竹两种菊花组成，此式纹样为经典祝寿花卉，故此类纹饰应作为宫廷寿诞之用。

Qing DYNASTY, YONGZHENG MARK AND PERIOD

A FINE DOUCAI CHRYSANTHEMUM AND LONGEVITY PATTERN PLATE Diameter: 20 cm

This plate, characterized by a chrysanthemum embracing longevity pattern at its center and six clusters of folded-branch chrysanthemums on the outer wall, interspersed with interlocking patterns, embodies the aesthetic pinnacle of the Yongzheng era. Similar patterns can also be found on bowls, meipings, ruyi ear garlic head vases, and other vessel shapes, all hallmarks of Yongzheng period pieces. The decorative color fill is precise, with a dense layout, and the chrysanthemums are rendered with multiple layers of color, portraying a Western decorative style with curled leaf edges, a realistic shadow and texture contrast. The base is inscribed in underglaze blue with “Da Qing Yongle Nian Zhi” (Made in the Great Qing Yongzheng Year) in regular script. The chrysanthemums, depicted both inside and outside the plate, are classic emblems of birthday blessings. Therefore, such patterns were often utilized for imperial birthday celebrations.

清 雍正

斗彩海屋添筹图盘 直径：20.9 厘米

大清雍正年制（六字双行楷书款）

“海屋添筹”典故出自宋·苏轼《东坡志林·三老语》，寓祝长寿之意。此为清宫御瓷重要的吉祥纹样之一，。

是器敞口，浅腹，圈足，器形周正。盘心以斗彩绘《海屋添筹图》，为宫廷寿诞用器。仙山楼阁，仙鹤填筹，福、禄、寿三星，寓“祝福长寿”之意，外壁绘蝙蝠、山石、灵芝、海水纹。是器画笔精美，设色淡雅而质感逼真，仙境之态随笔而至，乃生平所念最佳之胜景处，其所构建出之意境为帝王所喜。

QING DYNASTY, YONGZHENG MARK AND PERIOD

A RARE DOUCAI "IMMORTALS" DISH Diameter: 20.9 cm

The phrase "Hai Wu Tian Chou" originates from an anecdote relayed by Su Shi, the renowned Song Dynasty scholar, in his work *Dongpo Zhilin - San Lao Yu*. It conveys aspirations for a long life and is a coveted theme in imperial porcelain design.

This particular plate, characterized by its expansive mouth, shallow basin, and ringed base, displays a doucai rendition of the "Hai Wu Tian Chou" narrative, intended for use in imperial birthday rites. The composition is richly detailed, featuring divine palaces, transcendent cranes, and the auspicious "Three Star Gods" of Fu, Lu, and Shou—emblems of prosperity, status, and longevity, respectively. The plate's exterior is further adorned with auspicious bats, rugged rocks, lingzhi mushrooms, and stylized sea waves. Employing the doucai method, a harmonious fusion of underglaze blue and vibrant overglaze enamels, the piece radiates an air of refinement. Its precise brushstrokes and tasteful use of color reflect the heights of imperial porcelain artistry in the Yongzheng era, making it a testament to the period's sophisticated ceramic techniques.

清 雍正

斗彩如意云龙纹盘

直径：17.1 厘米

大清雍正年制（六字双行楷书款）

中国人自古将龙视之为祥瑞。“龙，鳞虫之长，能幽能明，能细能巨，能长能短。春分而登天，秋分而潜渊”，因此龙常与云气纹、火焰纹、海水纹衬托配合出现在器物上，以示其登天潜渊之特性。

是器盘心青花双圈内以斗彩绘侧面火珠立龙纹，形态生动，富于变化，细颈五爪，矫健有力。圈外簇拥“壬”字五彩云五朵，外壁呼应盘心，绘八朵五彩“品”字形云纹和卷云纹相间，下部绘海水纹，海波滚滚，有一浪卷起千堆雪之气势，描摹细腻，极富动感。是器云纹描绘极有特色，以青花细线勾勒轮廓，再填以各色彩料，红、黄、绿，色彩缤纷，形态飘逸。此种连绵不绝的云纹见于雍正御窑斗彩器，为雍正时期标准“五色祥云纹”。

QING DYNASTY, YONGZHENG MARK AND PERIOD

A VERY RARE DOUCAI “DRAGON” DISH

Diameter: 17.1 cm

This dish exhibits a central medallion outlined in blue-and-white, enclosing a side-faced dragon in Doucai palette chasing a flaming pearl. The dragon with a slender neck and five claws is robust and vigorous. Surrounding the medallion are five colorful extended clouds on the cavetto. The exterior wall features eight multi-colored cloud motifs alternating with scroll clouds, above a section of delicate wave patterns depicting rolling sea waves. Outlined in fine underglaze blue lines, the cloud motifs are distinctively filled with red, yellow, and green enamels, embodying a lively and elegant aesthetic. This continuous cloud motif is a standard "five-colored auspicious cloud motif" of the Yongzheng period, seen on Yongzheng imperial kiln doucai wares. The base is inscribed in underglaze blue with Yongzheng six-character reign mark in regular script.

清 雍正

斗彩绿龙纹盘 直径：21 厘米

大清雍正年制（六字双行楷书款）

此盘器形周正，胎质上乘，釉面莹润如玉。通体纹饰以青花勾勒轮廓，釉上绿彩描绘细节，历二次烧制而成。内外口沿均以青花绘双弦纹，盘心于双圈内绘立龙纹，虬髯飘逸，叱口突目，躯肢怒张，外壁绘双龙赶珠纹，极富动感，四周衬以火珠及云焰。整器画工精致流畅，施彩细腻柔和，绿彩厚澜翠莹，为雍正一朝独有之纤巧。

QING DYNASTY, YONGZHENG MARK AND PERIOD

A FINE AND RARE UNDERGLAZE-BLUE AND GREEN-ENAMELLED "DRAGON" DISH Diameter: 21 cm

This dish showcases superior clay quality and a jade-like glaze. The decoration is outlined in blue underglaze, with overglaze green enamel depicting details, achieved through a two-step firing process. Both inner and outer rims are adorned with double-line underglaze blue patterns. A majestic dragon motif at the center of the dish is dipicted within double circles. The dragon, with flowing whiskers and a ferocious stance, brings a dynamic vibe. The outer wall portrays a scene of double dragons chasing a flaming pearl, surrounded by fiery beads and cloud motifs. The artistry is refined and fluent, with delicate and soft color application, showcasing the rich and flowing green enamel distinctive of the meticulous craftsmanship unique to the Yongzheng period.

The base is inscribed with "Da Qing Yongzheng Nian Zhi" (Made in the reign of Yongzheng in the Great Qing Dynasty), consisting of six characters in two columns in regular script.

清 雍正

釉里红三鱼纹盘一对 直径：15 厘米 ×2

大清雍正年制（六字双行楷书款）

是器敞口，浅腹，圈足。内壁光素，外壁绘以釉里红三鱼纹，恣意潜游，别有意趣。所施白釉洁白温润，抚之如玉。釉里红纹饰为剪影式，不加细节描绘，三鱼色调红艳，凸现于白釉之上，相映成趣，悦目怡神。

此种釉里红制法承袭自永、宣御窑，所饰铜红釉，或夹施于透明釉层之间，异于常见之釉下铜红彩绘技艺。此法若成，所得红色更显强烈，虽无法呈递纹样细节，然具有红宝石般光泽，最适凸显剪影视效，文献称之为“釉里红宝烧”。

QING DYNASTY, YONGZHENG MARK AND PERIOD

A FINE PAIR OF COPPER-RED DECORATED “THREE-FISH” DISHES Diameter: 15 cmx2

The plates feature wide mouths, shallow bellies, and ring feet. The inner wall is smooth and plain, while the outer wall is adorned with an underglaze copper-red pattern of three fish whimsically swimming about, presenting a unique charm. The applied white glaze is pure, warm, and smooth to touch, reminiscent of jade. The underglaze red pattern is rendered in silhouette, without intricate detailing, where the vibrant red hue of the three fish stands out against the white glaze, creating a delightful and serene aesthetic. The base is marked in blue underglaze with the characters denoting the Yongzheng period of the Great Qing Dynasty in regular script.

This particular underglaze red technique is inherited from the imperial kilns of the Yongle and Xuande period. The copper-red glaze, sometimes layered within a clear glaze, differs from the commonly seen underglaze red painting artistry. When successful, this method yields a more intense red color, although it doesn't allow for detailed pattern rendering. Yet, it provides a ruby-like luster, making it ideal for silhouette visual effects.

大清雍
正年製
2163
大清雍
正年製
2163

YIZHENG GE PORCELAIN ALBUM

義正閣

清乾隆

QING DYNASTY, QIANLONG PERIOD

清 乾隆

青花釉里红狮滚绣球纹尊 高：32.9 厘米

大清乾隆年制（六字三行篆书款）

“瑞狮戏球”为古代艺术品喜闻乐见之纹饰，尤得皇家珍爱，在瓷器上以明代宣、成二朝官窑狮球碗、罐最为著称，而以青花釉里红来装饰狮球纹则为乾隆朝的首创。

是器瓶口外撇，束颈丰肩，腹下渐收。瓶身青花色泽浓艳，釉里红则略见淡雅。颈部饰一圈夔龙变形雷纹，肩处绘蝙蝠纹，近足处饰一圈仰莲瓣纹。腹部绘三狮滚绣球，一狮仰首顶球，一狮回首扑球，一狮前趋追球，以青花绘头尾眼睛，以釉里红绘狮身毛发；以青花绘飘带，以釉里红绘火焰，红蓝相间，互为辉映。其用笔精细，对三狮之刻画纤毫毕露，毛发茸茸之感尽现眼前，神态憨拙逼真。

此瓶据底款书写风格，推断其应为雍乾年间督陶官唐英之榷陶佳作。底款“乾”字中以“由”代“日”之写法，当属乾隆早期之物，且多作为青花釉里红器之底款。

QING DYNASTY, QIANLONG MARK AND PERIOD

A FINE AND VERY RARE UNDERGLAZE-BLUE AND COPPER-RED "LION" VASE Height: 32.9cm

The motif of lions playing with balls, cherished in ancient art, especially adored by royalty, was notably depicted on porcelain during the Xuande and Chenghua periods of the Ming Dynasty. The lions' heads, tails, eyes and fluttering ribbons are outlined in underglaze blue, while the underglaze red depicts the fur and the flames, creating a vibrant contrast.

This vase exhibits a flared mouth, constrained neck, full shoulders, tapering to the base. The body displays a vibrant blue and white palette, with subtle underglaze red. The neck is adorned with a Kui dragon thunder pattern, the shoulders with bat motifs, and near the base, upturned lotus petal motifs. The belly portrays three lions frolicking with embroidered balls; one touching the ball with its head up, one pouncing, and one chasing the ball. The lions' heads, tails, and eyes are outlined in blue underglaze, while the underglaze red depicts the fur; blue and white are used for the fluttering ribbons, and underglaze red for the flames, creating a vibrant contrast. The meticulous brushwork captures every strand of the lions' fur and their naive expressions exquisitely.

Based on the base marking style, it's speculated this vase is a fine work of porcelain superintendent Tang Ying during the Yongzheng to Qianlong periods. The character qian (乾) in the mark is filled by 由 instead of 日 ,which provides evidence that this piece was made at early stage of Qianlong period. It is often marked on underglaze blue and copper red wares.

清平樂

詠乾隆青花釉里紅獅滾繡球紋尊

銀尊暎月　光涵其表裏
紅蝠翻雲獅戲舞　八寶繡球伶俐
古瓶可盛稠酒　亦可斜簪木樨
太白潘越遺風　花酒由來一氣

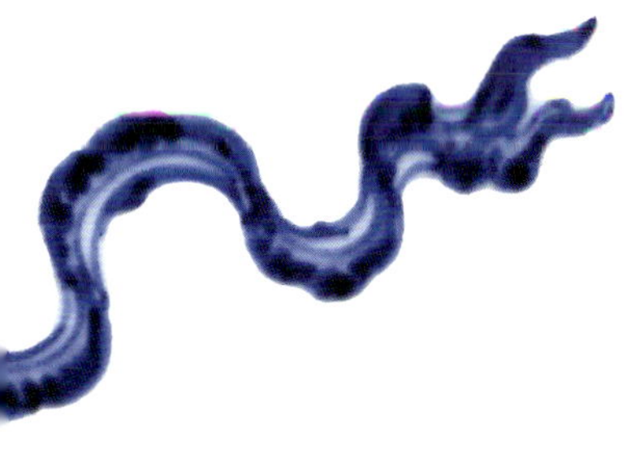

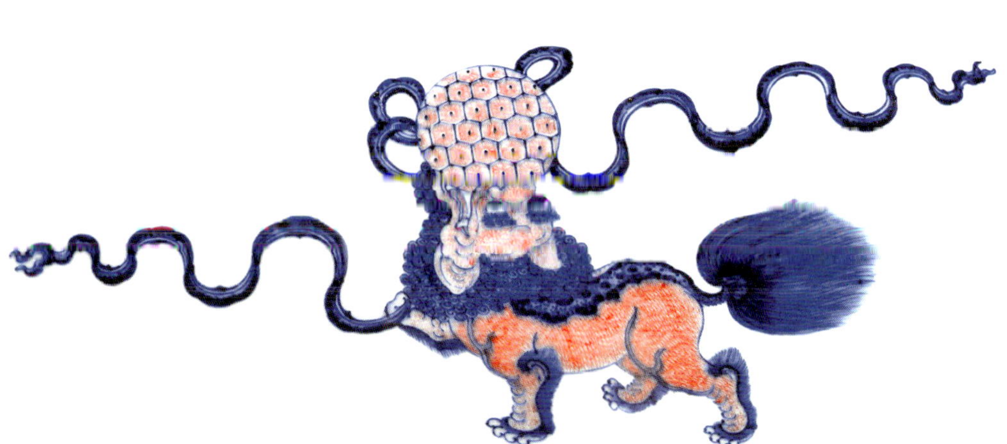

清 乾隆

青花缠枝番莲寿字纹如意尊 高：23.2 厘米

大清乾隆年制（六字三行篆书款）

《饮流斋说瓷·说瓶罐第七》记述："如意尊高约六七寸……清初多作青花，若纯色釉及暗花者，亦为雅制。"如意耳瓶，旧称如意尊，为雍窑新出器样。

是器口呈蒜头状，束颈，腰间内收，饰以凸棱一道，圆腹下部丰硕，器身因两侧置对称如意耳，故称"如意尊"。器身绘缠枝番莲纹，辅以回纹、如意纹、莲瓣纹等。花心处绘一"寿"字纹饰，十分罕见。此尊所绘莲纹自然流畅，层层递进，疏密有致，浓淡相宜。底青花书"大清乾隆年制"篆书款。此尊青花发色浓妍，瓷质之润，釉色之晶莹，历数百载而常新。

QING DYNASTY, QIANLONG MARK AND PERIOD

A FINE AND VERY RARE BLUE-AND WHITE DOUBLE-GOURD VASE

Height: 23.2cm

The "Ruyi" vase, traditionally called "Ruyi Zun", is recorded in *Yin Liu Zhai Shuo Ci* (On Ceramics by Yin Liu Zhai) representing a design evolution from the Yongzheng kilns.

Featuring a garlic-head shaped mouth, narrow neck, and indented waist adorned with a raised ridge, it leads to a full lower body. The name derives from the symmetrical ruyi handles on either side of the vessel. Decorated with scrolling lotus motifs, complemented by spiral, ruyi, and lotus petal designs. the piece features a character of shou (longevity) delicately painted at each flower's center. The lotus motifs exhibit a natural flow, organized in layers with balanced density and color intensity variations. The base inscribes the seal script mark "Da Qing Qianlong Nian Zhi" (Made during the Qianlong era of the Great Qing) in underglaze blue. The robust blue-and-white color, smooth porcelain quality, and crystalline glaze have retained a fresh appearance over centuries.

清 乾隆

青花双龙捧寿纹如意耳葫芦扁瓶一对 高：17.6 厘米 ×2

大清乾隆年制（六字三行篆书款）

是器为扁葫芦式造型，小器大样。肩颈处置对称绶带如意双耳。此式葫芦瓶极为罕有，是为乾隆朝御瓷之创新式样。颈部与胫部分绘青花花叶纹及曲折纹，外壁纹饰随形而绘，主题纹样为青花双龙捧“寿”纹，龙首位于瓶之下腹部，龙尾上摆至肩部，双龙尾部分叉，状若卷草。周身围绕一团蝠纹，气势威严，对称而为，寓意“福寿双全”，至为吉祥。底青花书“大清乾隆年制”篆书款。是器以龙纹体现皇权，且是以图案谐音“福”“寿”之美好寓意集于一身的宫廷陈设器。

QING DYNASTY, QIANLONG MARK AND PERIOD

A PAIR OF BLUE AND WHITE DRAGON DOUBLE-GOURD VASES Height: 17.6 cm ×2

These vases are crafted in a flattened gourd silhouette, showcasing the grandeur of a small object. At the shoulder and neck, symmetrically placed are ruyi ears, making this particular style of gourd vase exceedingly rare and a novel design of the imperial porcelain during the Qianlong period. The neck and base are adorned with blue-and-white floral and twisted patterns, with the external decorative scheme following the form of the vases. The central theme displays blue-and-white double dragons bearing the symbol of shou (longevity), with the dragon heads located at the lower belly of the vases and the tails extending upwards to the shoulders. The tails of the dragons bifurcate, resembling curled grass. Enriching the entirety are bat motifs systematically placed, emanating a majestic aura. It symbolizes holding both happiness and longevity, which is an auspicious omen in ancient times. The base of the vases is inscribed with Qianlong six-character reign mark in underglaze blue seal script. Through the dragon motif, the vases embody imperial authority, while the phonetic harmony of “Fu” (happiness) and “Shou” (longevity) in the design encapsulates auspicious wishes, making it a royal decorative artifact.

清 乾隆

粉彩云龙纹笔 长：17.1 厘米

大清乾隆年制（六字三行篆书款）

明清两代，御用制笔工艺极为考究。《陈设档》宣统二年（1910）：“懋勤殿现存陈设库存”载有“磁笔管十四枝”。档案所载“磁笔管”数量稀少，极为珍罕。

是器末端制为椭圆球状，管身稍细，近笔首处制为覆斗状，造型修长，灵巧秀气。外壁以粉彩为饰，整器周身遍布祥云，五彩缤纷，耀目异常。龙纹随管身盘旋而出，以矾红描金绘就，龙身盘旋而降，所绘至为细腻，龙身细节交代清晰，龙翔云间，极其潇洒，富皇家威仪之感，颇具气势。

著录于钱振宗主编：《清代瓷器赏鉴》，中华书局（香港）有限公司、上海科学技术出版社，1997 年，第 184 页，图 245。

QING DYNASTY, QIANLONG MARK AND PERIOD

A FINE AND RARE FAMILLE-ROSE "DRAGON" BRUSH

Long: 17.1 cm

The Ming and Qing Dynasties represented an epoch of meticulous artisanship in the creation of imperial brushes. An archival document from the second year of Xuantong's reign (1910) titled *Furniture Archive* reveals that the "Maoqin Palace currently holds in storage 14 ceramic brush shafts". The recorded quantity of "ceramic brush shafts" is scarce, rendering them exceedingly rare treasures.

This brush features an elliptical ball terminus with a slender shaft body that transitions into a flared shape near the head in an elegant form. Adorned with pink famille-rose enamels, it's enveloped in auspicious clouds with a golden dragon motif spiraling along the shaft, meticulously outlined in iron-red. The dragon, finely detailed, soars amidst the clouds, embodying royal dignity and exuding a commanding presence. The end of the brush shaft is marked with the iron-red inscription "Da Qing Qianlong Nian Zhi" (Made during Qianlong ear of the Qing Dynasty) in seal script.

Literature: Qian Zhenzong, *Qing Dai Ci Qi Jian Shang* (Appreciation of Qing Dynasty Porcelain), Chung Hwa Book Company (Hong Kong) Limited. and Shanghai Scientific and Technical Publishers, 1997, p. 184, pl. 245.

清 乾隆

釉里红喜上眉梢图如意耳抱月瓶 高：17.8 厘米

大清乾隆年制（六字三行篆书款）

抱月瓶又名“宝月瓶”“马褂瓶”，其器形源自西亚金属器，盛行于明初永、宣两朝，清代雍乾御窑继有追摹之作。而釉里红纹饰则为乾隆御窑慕古创新之作。

是器直口，细颈，扁圆腹，椭圆形圈足，颈肩处饰如意形双耳。通体釉里红为饰，口沿外饰双弦纹，颈绘竹叶纹，腹部绘《喜上眉梢图》，繁花山石之间，两只喜鹊正回首凝望，一翎一羽，神态毕现。梅花竞相绽放，花瓣轻透、娇嫩欲滴，繁盛中更显雅致，呈现一派春光明媚景象。所施釉里红一色妍丽而不炫，恰如其分，含蓄之美宛若佳人初醉。腹上下以缠枝花一周作边饰。

是器与永乐原型相较，纹饰格局更为复杂，且颇有创新，但画工仍严谨细腻。釉里红所绘纹饰已有光影效果，阴阳相分，明暗有致，层次分明。

此器为丁韪良的后人所有。丁韪良生于印度（1827），后至中国（1850），是同文馆的总教习（1869—1895），由光绪皇帝指任为京师大学堂第一任总教习（1898）。此器世代相传，为其曾孙所有。

QING DYNASTY, QIANLONG MARK AND PERIOD

A RARE UNDERGLAZE-RED “'MAGPIE AND PRUNUS” MOONFLASK Height: 17.8 cm

This Moonflask, also termed “Baoyue Vase” or “Magua Vase”, originated from Western Asian metallic ware, popularized in early Ming Dynasty, continuing through Yongzheng and Qianlong eras of the Qing Dynasty. The underglaze red motif here reflects the Qianlong imperial kiln's admiration for antiquity fused with innovation.

The vessel sports a straight mouth, slender neck, flat round belly, and oval foot ring, with a pair of ruyi handles at the neck-shoulder junction. Decorated entirely in underglaze red, it features a double-string motif around the mouth rim, bamboo leaf patterns on the neck, and a delightful scene on the belly: amid flourishing blooms and rocky terrain, two magpies look back at each other, with their plumage captured meticulously. The blooming plum blossoms add to the elegance, showing a picturesque spring scene. The red underglaze, exquisite yet not ostentatious. Entwined flower branches border the belly's upper and lower sections. On the base, underglaze blue characters inscribe “Da Qing Qianlong Nian Zhi” (Made during Qianlong ere of the Qing Dynasty) in seal script.

This piece belongs to William Alexander Parsons Martin's lineage, born in Indiana (1827), moved to China (1850), and became Tongwenguan’s President (1869-1865). He worked as the inaugural president of the Imperial University of Peking (1898) as appointed by Emperor Guangxu. The vase, inherited for generations, came from his great-grandson.

清 乾隆

胭脂红地洋彩轧道锦上添花纹贯耳扁瓶 高：25.8 厘米

大清乾隆年制（六字三行篆书款）

“洋彩”为18世纪清宫与西洋文化交流互动而产生之艺术珍品，为雍乾时期清宫对运用西洋绘画技法描绘的彩瓷之正式名称。洋彩瓷器的成熟与流行，使得西洋技法与西洋题材在清宫瓷器上得到完美呈现。“洋彩”名称最早出现于雍正十三年（1735）唐英所撰之《陶务叙略碑记》：“洋彩器皿，本朝新仿西洋珐琅画法，人物、山水、花卉、翎毛，无不精细入神。”

是器直口，贯耳，溜肩鼓腹，圈足。器身以胭脂红彩为地，通体轧道卷草纹。主体绘胭脂红地锦上添花纹，颈部为黄地花卉，双耳以白地蓝料花卉装饰。口沿处饰如意云头一周，近足处饰仰莲瓣一周。画面繁而不乱，巧夺天工，美艳至极。外底施松石绿釉。

著录于首都博物馆编：《香江雅集——香港回归祖国二十周年特展》，北京：文物出版社，2018年，181页，图版188号。

QING DYNASTY, QIANLONG MARK AND PERIOD

A YANGCAI RUBY-GROUND SGRAFFITO LOTUS VASE

Height: 25.8 cm

Yangcai emerged from the cultural exchanges between the Qing Palace and the west during the 18th century, featuring colored porcelain painted using Western techniques in the Yongzheng-Qianlong era. This vessel has a straight mouth, loop handles, sloping shoulders, a bulging belly, and a ring foot. It's adorned with sgraffito scrolled foliage on a rouge red ground. The main body displays a jinshang tianhua (adding flowers to the brocade) motif, (Adding Flowers to the Brocade) motif, the neck features a yellow ground with floral design, and the handles are decorated with blue-enamelled flowers on a white ground. The rim and near foot are ornamented with ruyi cloud and upward lotus petal designs respectively. The exterior bottom is celadon green-glazed with a red “Da Qing Qianlong Nian Zhi” (Made during Qianlong era of the Qing Dynasty) seal mark in the center.

Literature: *Treasures of Hong Kong: The 20th Anniversary of Hong Kong's Handover,* Capital Museum, Beijing, 2018, p. 181, pl. 188.

清 乾隆

松绿地粉彩缠枝莲纹五子登科包袱瓶 高：42 厘米

大清乾隆年制（六字三行篆书款）

“五子登科”出自《宋史·窦仪传》，后成为中国传统吉祥图案。明清时亦有“状元及第，五子登科”之说法。

是器整体为包袱形。一条红色锦地丝带将瓶身分为上下两层，缠枝莲纹作平面主题纹饰，瑞蝠纹点缀其间。缠枝莲枝蔓绵绵中祥蝠飞舞，寓意乾隆时期的太平盛世与吉祥之意。纹饰均以金彩勾边，工艺之精，叹为观止。五个动作各异之瓷塑童子，或手捧如意，或手持寿桃，或手拿竹笙，或攀爬嬉戏，描绘了一幅生动的五子登科场景。人物细腻生动，布局合理，完美地展示出乾隆朝制瓷的最高水平。底部金彩书“大清乾隆年制”篆书款。乾隆年制之包袱形瓷器，异常罕见。此器器形、纹饰，举世无双，是为孤例。

QING DYNASTY, QIANLONG MARK AND PERIOD

A VERY RARE PINE TURQUOISE GROUND FAMILLE ROSE "FIVE SCHOLARS ATTAINING SCHOLARLY HONORS" POUCH-SHAPED VASE Height: 42 cm

The depiction of five boys on the present vase is particularly auspicious, as it signifies the saying wuzi dengke (five sons attaining scholarly honors), which originates from *History of the Song Dynasty-Biography of Dou Yi*. It refers to the supreme achievement of one family whose five sons passed the civil service examination. The ovoid body rising to a tall neck and supported on a short foot, with five boys clambering over the vase. A ribbon tied sash enameled in tones of iron red decorated at the shoulder divides the body of the vase into upper and lower sections. The twined lotus pattern serves as the primary flat pattern decoration, with bat patterns interspersed within. Amidst the meandering twined lotus stems, auspicious bats flutter, symbolizing the peace and prosperity during the Qianlong period. The patterns are outlined in gold, a testament to the exquisite craftsmanship, leaving one in awe. Five porcelain figurines with distinct postures, one holding a Ruyi scepter, one holding peaches of longevity, one holding bamboo musical instruments, and others climbing and playing, vividly depict the scene of 'Five Sons Attaining Scholarly Honors.' The characters are delicately crafted, logically arranged, showcasing the pinnacle of porcelain craftsmanship during the Qianlong era. The base of the vase is marked with "Da Qing Qianlong Nian Zhi" (Made in the Qianlong era of the Great Qing) in gold seal script, highlighting its historical significance. Porcelain pieces with a pouch pattern from the Qianlong period are exceedingly rare. The unique form and designs of this vase render it unparalleled.

滿庭芳

詠乾隆松綠地粉彩五子登科包袱瓶

金縷青碧 香凝瑞彩

百子鼎沸華堂

東風得意 青雲路穩

要識登科次第

待看那北斗光芒

古今少 建安諸子

錦繡好文章

清 乾隆

粉彩仿掐丝珐琅番莲福寿纹双龙耳瓶 高：34 厘米

乾隆对铜胎掐丝珐琅器尤为钟爱，尝下命以瓷仿效。彼时工艺精湛，仿学艺作近乎完美，时出几可乱真之品。画师在器身上以描金勾勒，妙仿景泰蓝上之鎏金铜丝，流丽线条，对比鲜明，赏心悦目。

是器珍罕独特，他例无寻，并无相近作例记载，是为孤例。整器尊贵秀美，装饰雍容华丽，通体施松石绿釉为地，色泽清丽，纯净空灵。颈部及腹部绘花卉纹，形态各异，摇曳动人，落英缤纷。此器以松石绿釉摹铜胎掐丝珐琅之色地，以金彩勾勒替换掐丝，色地纹饰繁密，风格上更接近于洋彩瓷作。

QING DYNASTY, QIANLONG PERIOD

A VERY RARE FAMILLE-ROSE CLOISONNE-IMITATION BOTTLE VASE Height: 34 cm

During Emperor Qianlong's reign, a deep appreciation for cloisonné enamel wares led to an order to replicate these using porcelain. The era's craftsmanship was outstanding, with imitation techniques producing pieces nearly indistinguishable from real enamels. Artists used gilded outlines to emulate the gilded copper wires of Jingtai blue cloisonnés, creating elegant and contrasting lines that were aesthetically pleasing.

This singular master piece is unique and rare, with no similar examples found. The vase exudes nobility and elegance, adorned with opulent decorations. It's glazed with turquoise green, presenting a clear and ethereal aesthetic. The neck and belly are embellished with diverse floral motifs, shedding delightful petals. The base is inscribed with “Da Qing Qianlong Nian Zhi” (Made during the Qianlong period of the Great Qing) in underglaze blue. The turquoise green glaze mimics the color of copper-bodied cloisonné enamel, with gold-colored outlines substituting for cloisonne wires, closely resembling Yangcai porcelain works. This artifact showcases a blend of Chinese craftsmanship with a touch of Western aesthetic influence. It represents a significant period of artistic evolution in the Qing Dynasty, making it a pivotal subject for connoisseurs and enthusiasts of Chinese porcelain artistry.

清 乾隆

仿雕漆珊瑚红地描金瑞蝠穿云游龙纹帽架 高：26.5 厘米

仿雕漆釉指在器身施以朱红釉，并以雕刻表现纹饰，其效果与漆器中的剔红无异，被称为“仿漆釉”。其摹仿之肖，无论造型、颜色或质感，均极近漆器。

此帽架由三部分构成，上部帽托为球状；中部柱身四周等距出戟；下部底座四周等距塑四夔凤，凤体蜿蜒，昂首张口，身形柔美灵动。通身浮雕云蝠、如意云头、锦地花卉及云龙纹，各层纹饰之间均有辅助纹饰相隔，设色艳丽华美，代表了其时仿漆雕瓷技艺之最高水平。此器成型复杂，由于不能拉坯只能靠拼合方成，故在烧造中极易疵裂变形，因此传世品稀少。

QING DYNASTY, QIANLONG PERIOD

A VERY RARE IMITATION-LACQUER "DRAGON" PORCELAIN HAT STAND Height: 26.5 cm

The imitation of carved lacquer glaze technique refers to the application of a vermilion glaze on the porcelain body, with carved decorations to mimic the effect found in carved lacquerware. The degree of resemblance it bears, be it in form, color, or texture, is remarkably close to actual lacquerware. This hat stand comprises three parts: the upper hat holder is spherical in shape, the middle column features evenly spaced flanges around its circumference; the lower base also has evenly spaced, molded mythical Kui Phoenix figures, with their bodies winding gracefully, heads holding high and mouths open, which embodies a sense of beauty and agility. The whole body of the hat stand is elaborately embossed with motifs of auspicious bats, ruyi cloud, flowers, and cloud dragons. Each layer of decoration is separated by auxiliary patterns, rendering a vivid and extravagant color palette, representing the pinnacle of imitation carved lacquer ceramic artistry of the time. The complex molding of this artifact, due to its inability to be wheel-thrown and thus requiring assembly, makes it prone to cracks and deformations during the firing process. Therefore, the extant pieces are rare.

清 乾隆

粉青釉刻螭龙纹盘口纸槌瓶 高：9.8 厘米

大清乾隆年制（六字三行篆书款）

纸槌瓶为宋代官窑创制。制作原始，仅为容器，且无“纸槌”之名，而统以“官窑瓶”称之。明代晚期，尚雅嗜古之士大夫才为该瓶取名“纸槌”，并一直沿用至今。而其也由最初的盛装器演化为花事用具。

青釉美瓷备受乾隆宫廷钟睐，然于釉下雕刻纹饰则为新举。是器盘口，直颈，折肩，卧足，通体施粉青釉，釉下模印纹饰，颈部饰变体蕉叶纹，肩部及腹部饰仿古夔龙纹饰，所刻龙纹吮口突目，翎羽飞扬。间以回纹及鼓钉纹相隔，华美异常。本品釉色清澈透净，宛若宋时龙泉青瓷，底施粉青釉。

QING DYNASTY, QIANLONG MARK AND PERIOD

A CELADON GLAZE "DRAGON" MALLET SHAPE VASE

Height: 9.8 cm

Originating from Song Dynasty official kilns, the Mallet Shape Vase initially served as a simple container, known as "official kiln vase". The name "Paper Mallet" was coined by antiquity-admiring scholars during the late Ming Dynasty, and it was used as a floral vessel over time. The Qianlong court held a deep appreciation for celadon glazed porcelain. However, engraving designs beneath the glaze was a novel practice. This vase, with a dish mouth, round body, folded shoulders, and a flat base, is adorned with a pale celadon glaze. Beneath the glaze, engraved motifs are meticulously executed. The neck displays a variant banana leaf motif, while the shoulder and body exhibit an ancient-style Chi dragon design. The engraved dragons, depicted with open mouths and protruding eyes, are interspersed with wave patterns and stud designs, creating a lavish aesthetic. The crystalline and pure glaze echoes the elegance of Longquan celadon ware in the Song Dynasty showcasing the refined porcelain craftsmanship of the Qianlong period.

清 乾隆

粉青釉弦纹高足杯 高：9.6 厘米

大清乾隆年制（六字单行篆书款）

是器撇口，深弧腹及底内收，腹中部及胫部起凸弦纹，下承外撇式高圈足，胎体坚白细糯。通体施粉青釉，釉面清润莹洁，宛若隐青之色。足底以青花书“大清乾隆年制”六字单行篆书款。是器造型简洁素雅，通体釉色青翠欲滴，弦纹装饰则起到了均衡协调之作用，使得单一的釉色增加了韵律感，实得文人雅致淡然旨趣。

著录于罗伯特·雅各布森，叶佩兰，朱汤生：《清代康雍乾宫窑瓷器：望星楼藏瓷》，香港，2004 年，204—205 页，图版 77 号。

展览：借展明尼阿波利斯美术馆，2003—2020 年。

QING DYNASTY, QIANLONG MARK AND PERIOD

A FINE STEMBOWL WITH PALE BLUISH-GREEN CELADON GLAZE Height: 9.6 cm

The porcelain piece features a flared mouth, deep arced belly, and an inward-curving base. The middle of the belly and the lower body is decorated with protruding string patterns, supported by a tall, outward-flaring ring foot. The body of the porcelain is firm, white, and finely textured. A pale celadon glaze is applied all over, with the glaze surface being clear, lustrous, and glossy, resembling the color of hidden green. The base of the foot is marked with “Da Qing Qianlong Nian Zhi” (Made during the Qianlong era of the Great Qing) in blue underglaze, in a single-line seal script. This piece showcases a simple and elegant form, with the entire body exuding a verdant allure. The string pattern decoration plays a role in balancing and harmonizing the piece, adding rhythm to the singular glaze color, thereby capturing the essence of scholarly elegance and understated beauty.

Literature: Robert Jacobsen, Ye Peilan and Julian Thompson, *Imperial Perfection – The Palace Porcelain of Three Emperors: Kangxi - Yongzheng - Qianlong,* Hong Kong, 2004, p. 204-205, pl. 77.

Exhibited: On loan exhibition to the Minneapolis Institute of Art, USA, 2003-2020.

清 乾隆

仿汝釉出戟花觚 高：17 厘米

大清乾隆年制（六字三行篆书款）

觚原为商周时期之重要酒器，后世转为插花之用，故有“花觚”之名。是器作三段式，小器大样。喇叭形口，腹部鼓出，足胫外撇，腹部、足胫均出四道棱戟，古朴大方。通体施仿汝釉，温润厚腴，色泽淡恬幽靓，器身满布细小开片，秀美天成。全器造型别致，俊秀挺拔，隽雅端丽，纯净釉色与古朴之器形完美结合，相得益彰，置于案头，意趣丛生，为书斋之雅器。

QING DYNASTY, QIANLONG MARK AND PERIOD

A FINE RU-TYPE VASE, HUAGU Height: 17 cm

Originally, the vase known as “Gu” was a significant wine vessel during the Shang and Zhou dynasties. Later it was adapted for flower arrangement, hence earning the name huagu (flower vase). This particular piece exhibits a three-segment design, embodying a grand style within a compact structure. It features a flared rim, a bulging belly, and outward-splayed foot, with four halberd-like ridges protruding from the belly and foot, exuding an aura of ancient simplicity and elegance. The entire vase is coated with an imitation Ru glaze, achieving a warm, thick, and graceful appearance. The glaze's color is tranquil, exuding a subtle beauty. Throughout the vase's body, tiny crackles are present, epitomizing a natural elegance. The unique form of the vase, slender and graceful, coupled with the pure glaze color and the ancient, simple shape, complement each other perfectly. When placed on a table, it invokes a sense of refined aesthetics, making it a desirable ornamental piece for a study room.

清 乾隆

浆胎仿定釉暗刻兽面纹盖碗尊 高：20.4 厘米

大清乾隆年制（六字三行篆书款）

此式盖碗尊为清代御窑经典样式，因口部造型与盖碗相似而得名，见有仿定白釉及青花品种。仿定白釉为乾隆朝所独有，较青花品种少之。

是器秀巧可爱，线条起伏丰富，胎体轻盈细白，透明釉清亮匀净，釉面开片，古意盎然，通体剔刻纹饰，自上而下装饰卷草纹、蕉叶纹、连珠纹、回纹作为辅助纹样，肩部饰相对式夔龙纹。层次丰富，过渡清晰，颈腹部皆有一道留白弦纹凸起，与瓶口外凸的造型相呼应，纹饰繁复精细，是为乾隆御窑仿定窑之隽品。底部中心刻“大清乾隆年制”篆书款。

张宗宪旧藏

QIANG DYNASTY, QIANLONG MARK AND PERIOD

A FINE AND RARE CREAMY-WHITE GLAZED SOFT-PASTE VASE

Height: 20.4 cm

This style of vase is a classic design from the Imperial Kilns during the Qing Dynasty, named for its resemblance in form to a covered bowl at the mouth. Variations of this style are seen in imitation Ding ware with white glaze and blue-and-white porcelain. The imitation Ding white glaze is a distinctive feature of the Qianlong era, and is found less frequently compared to the blue-and-white varieties.

The vase is delicately exquisite, with flowing lines and a light, fine white body. The transparent glaze is clean, bright, and uniform, displaying a craze (fine crackle) that evokes a sense of antiquity. The entire vase is adorned with carved patterns, with scrolling foliage, banana leaf, bead, and spiral patterns serving as auxiliary decoration from top to bottom. On the shoulder, there are opposing Kui dragon patterns. The decoration is layered and transitions are clear, with a white string pattern protruding on both the neck and belly, resonating with the outward form of the vase mouth. The intricate and fine decoration marks this as a remarkable piece from the Qianlong Imperial Kilns imitating Ding Kilns. At the center of the bottom, the seal script "Da Qing Qianlong Nian Zhi" (Made during the Qianlong era of the Great Qing) is inscribed.

Collection of Robert Chang

清 乾隆

冬青釉刻缠枝牡丹纹长颈瓶 高：35 厘米

大清乾隆年制（六字三行篆书款）

是器直口，长颈，溜肩，鼓腹，圈足。器身刻缠枝牡丹纹，纹饰清晰利落。是器塑形静雅，粉青釉透亮莹润，精心构思亦施艺谨慎，然浑然天成，不带匠气。所刻牡丹纹瑰丽分明，取材自较为朴雅之元、明龙泉青釉器，瓶颈叶纹、瓶肩如意头等，以及粉青釉色，均为艺匠原创，以切合清宫喜好瑰丽繁华之品位。纹饰及釉色取灵感自浙江龙泉窑之器，是器器形则见新颖，迎合乾隆帝之喜好。

QING DYNASTY, QIANLONG MARK AND PERIOD

A RARE AND FINE CELADON ENAMELED PORCELAIN VASE WITH MOLDED DECORATION Height: 35 cm

This piece features a straight mouth, elongated neck, sloped shoulders, bulbous body, and ringed foot. The body of the vase is meticulously carved with intertwined peony motifs, the design being clear and crisp. The vase exudes a quiet elegance in its form; the celadon glaze is translucent and lustrous. Meticulously conceived and executed with precision, the piece exudes a natural finesse devoid of any artisanal ostentation. The carved peony motifs are vivid and luxurious, drawing inspiration from the more modest Yuan and Ming Dynasty Longquan celadon pieces. The leaf patterns on the neck, ruyi head motifs on the shoulders, as well as the celadon glaze, are all original creations by the artisan to cater to the Qing court's taste for opulence and extravagance. The design and glaze draw inspiration from the Zhejiang Longquan kiln pieces; The form of this vase offers a novel appeal aligning with Emperor Qianlong's preferences.

清 乾隆

仿官釉八卦琮式瓶 高：28厘米

大清乾隆年制（六字三行篆书款）

琮式瓶器形源自新石器时代之玉琮，作为瓷器造型则最早见于南宋。清代各朝延烧不衰，为清宫经典陈设用器。

是器器形规整，胎体厚重，四方形器身设圆形口和圈足，象征天圆地方。瓶身饰凸起八卦纹，线条挺括，满施粉青色仿官釉，釉面呈大小开片，更添古雅气韵。

陈玉阶旧藏

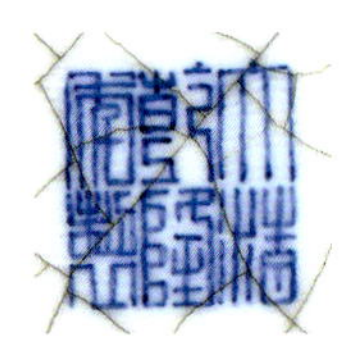

QING DYNASTY, QIANLONG MARK AND PERIOD

A FINE GE-TYPE GLAZED CONG-SHAPED VASE

Height: 28 cm

Originating from the jade cong of the Neolithic era, the cong-form in porcelain first appeared during the Southern Song Dynasty. This style continued to flourish throughout various reigns in the Qing Dynasty, and became a classic piece in the imperial palace.

The vase has a well-structured form with a hefty body. It adopts a square-shaped body with a circular mouth and foot, symbolizing the concept of "Heaven is round, Earth is square". The vase is adorned with raised Bagua (Eight Trigrams) motifs, presenting firm and well-defined lines. Covered entirely with a powder blue ge-type glaze, the surface exhibits crackles of varying sizes, adding to its antiquated charm.

Y.C. Chen Collection

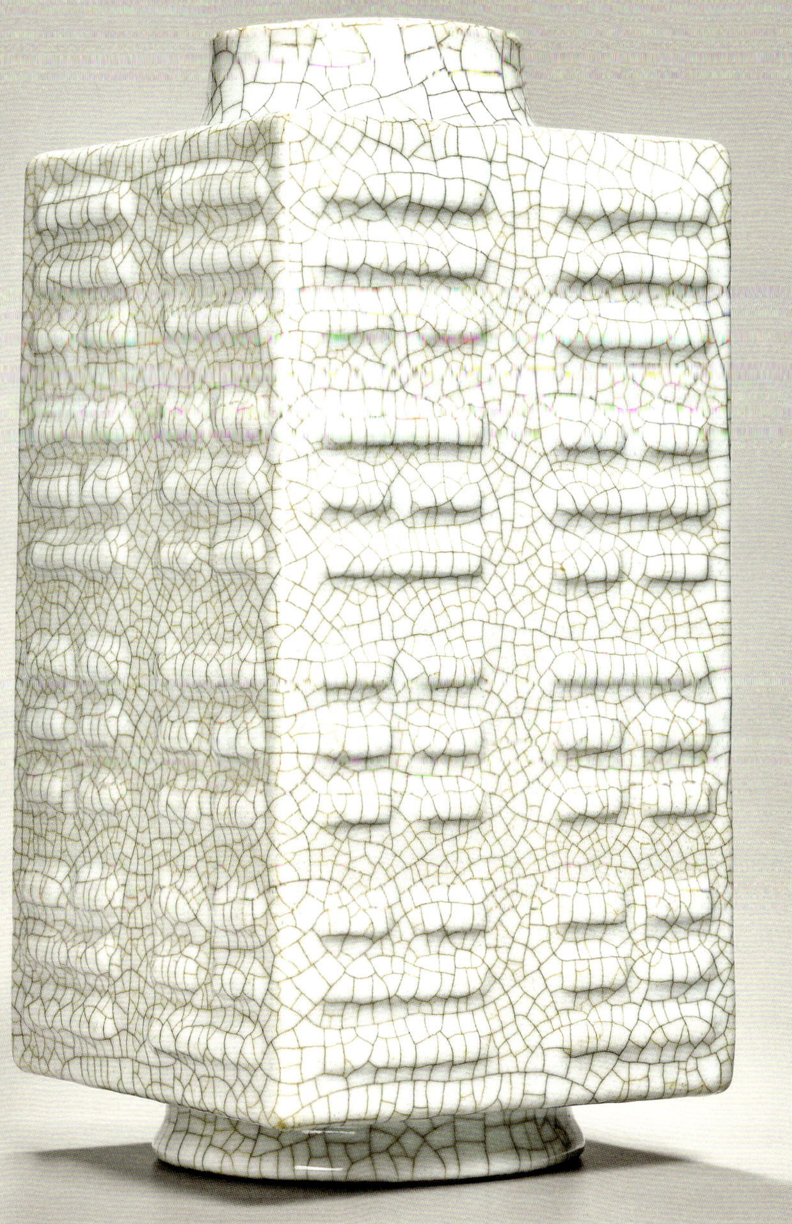

清 乾隆

炉钧釉灯笼瓶 高：24.3厘米

大清乾隆年制（六字三行篆书款）

灯笼瓶为清代创烧之瓷器新品，因形似灯笼而得名，传世所见有青花、粉彩、颜色釉等诸多品种。

是器口微外撇，短颈，长圆腹，底内收，下承圈足，器形简洁大方，亦不失华贵之气。瓶腹部两侧贴塑垂带耳，通体施炉钧釉，釉彩自然流淌，蓝、紫色交织熔融，似山岚缥缈、云气幻化，釉面五彩光晕清晰可见，极尽变幻之能事。

QING DYNASTY, QIANLONG MARK AND PERIOD

A ROBIN'S-EGG BLUE GLAZED LANTERN VASE

Height: 24.3 cm

The lantern vase is a novel ceramic creation of the Qing Dynasty, named for its resemblance to a lantern. Extant examples showcase a variety of designs including blue-and-white, famille-rose, and colored glazes.

This vase has a slightly flared rim, short neck, elongated round body, and an inward-curved base, standing on a ringed foot. Its simple and elegant shape exude a sense of luxury. On either side of the vase's body, flat ribbed handles are attached. It is fully glazed in a robin's-egg blue hue, with the glaze naturally flowing, intertwining blue and purple shades, evoking the imagery of mist-shrouded mountains and ethereal clouds. The multicolored luster of the glaze is clearly visible, showcasing a captivating display of changing colors. The base is incised with the seal script inscription "Da Qing Qianlong Nian Zhi" (Made during the Qianlong era of the Great Qing).

清 乾隆

青花八吉祥纹双龙耳抱月瓶 高：49.5 厘米

大清乾隆年制（六字三行篆书款）

八吉祥纹源出藏传佛教，作为吉祥图案装饰瓷器始于元代。是器直口，粗颈，扁圆腹，下置椭圆形圈足。颈肩饰双耳，又称云耳。腹部两面中心有圆状凸起。通体青花装饰，口沿处为回纹，颈部为缠枝花卉，腹部两面绘回纹一周，中心为朵花纹，外环以莲瓣纹内绘八吉祥纹，腹侧绘缠枝莲纹。是器庄重典雅，青花色泽纯正清丽，画工笔触严整而不失流畅之致，呈现清一代青花御制瓷器之神逸。

QING DYNASTY, QIANLONG MARK AND PERIOD

A SUPERB LARGE MING-STYLE BLUE AND WHITE "BAJIXIANG" MOONFLASK

Height: 49.5 cm

The motif of bajixiang (eight auspicious symbols) traces its roots to the Tibetan Buddhist tradition, introduced to central China during the Yuan dynasty, and adorning porcelain ware as auspicious decorative motifs began from that period. This vase features a straight mouth, a stout neck, a flattened circular body, and is set upon an oval-shaped foot ring. The neck is adorned with a pair of handles, also referred to as cloud handles. The center of both sides of the belly showcases a circular protrusion. The entire vase is decorated with blue-and-white designs. The rim of the mouth is adorned with scroll patterns. The neck showcases intertwined floral patterns, and a scroll pattern encircles the body, with a flower motif at the center. The outer ring is embellished with lotus petal motifs enclosing the Eight Auspicious Symbols. The sides of the belly are adorned with intertwined lotus patterns. This piece embodies a dignified elegance, with a pure and clear blue and white hue, and meticulous yet fluid brushwork, exemplifying the exalted essence of blue-and-white imperial porcelain from the Qing Dynasty.

清 乾隆

青花折枝花卉纹六方瓶 高：65.5 厘米

大清乾隆年制（六字三行篆书款）

六方瓶器形始创于雍正，盛于乾隆，见有青花、粉彩及单色釉品种。是器呈六方形，侈口长颈，折肩弧腹，圈足外撇作台阶状，端正大气，恢宏威严。胎质细腻，釉汁润泽，通体以青花描绘，发色苍翠。器物口沿、肩部及足胫分饰回纹、云雷纹及如意云头，器身起棱折角处则描绘卷草花卉。颈部六面分饰折枝花卉，腹部主体以“三多”为主题纹饰，绘制石榴、佛手、寿桃，寓意多子、多福、多寿，瑞果之间搭配菊花、牡丹、莲花三组折枝花卉，祥花瑞果，穷秀极妍，吉祥之气尽现。

QING DYNASTY, QIANLONG MARK AND PERIOD

AN EXCEPTIONALLY FINE AND MAGNIFICENT BLUE AND WHITE "SANDUO" HEXAGONAL VASE

Height: 65.5 cm

The hexagonal vase design originated during the Yongzheng era and flourished during the Qianlong reign, with variations seen in blue and white, famille rose, and monochrome glaze. This particular vase showcases a hexagonal form, flaunting a lavish mouth, elongated neck, folded shoulders, and curved body, all standing on a tiered base resembling steps, embodying a dignified, grand, and majestic aura. The vase is finely crafted with a smooth and lustrous glaze, meticulously adorned with blue and white patterns that exhibit a verdant hue. The rim, shoulder, and foot of the vase are decorated with spiral, cloud-thunder, and ruyi cloud patterns respectively, while the facets and angles of the body are painted with scrolling floral designs. The six facets of the neck feature branching floral patterns, and the main body of the vase is adorned with a sanduo (three abundance) theme. The depicting of pomegranates symbolizes abundant offspring, citrons represent abandunt blessings and peaches symbolize longevity. These auspicious fruits are interspersed with groups of chrysanthemum, peony, and lotus branching floral patterns, embodying a harmonious blend of auspicious flora and fruits, culminating in a display of refined elegance and propitious aura.

清 乾隆

青花缠枝西番莲团寿纹六方贯耳瓶 高：45厘米

大清乾隆年制（六字三行篆书款）

是器呈六方形，长颈，两侧饰对称贯耳。通体以青花绘缠枝莲为主题图案，其间衬以海水、如意头、变形莲瓣等纹。是器特殊之处在于瓶腹描绘大朵缠枝宝相花，且花心为团寿纹，象征福泽延绵、多福多寿，寓意吉祥，在同类器中少见。整器青花色彩艳丽，纹饰层次清晰，构图匀称。底青花书“大清乾隆年制”篆书款，篆法特殊，与一类雍正篆书款结字相类，当属乾隆早期所用。

QING DYNASTY, QIANLONG MARK AND PERIOD

A FINE BLUE-AND-WHITE “LOTUS SCROLL” HEXAGONAL VASE Height: 45 cm

The vase manifests a hexagonal body, elongated neck, and symmetric a pair of symmetric tubular handles on either side. The entire piece is decorated with a theme of underglaze blue lotus flowers entwined in branches, interspersed with patterns of wave patterns, ruyi heads, and stylized lotus petals. A distinctive feature of this vase lies in its depiction of a large entwined precious flower on the belly, with the core designed as a circular longevity symbol, emblematic of enduring blessings, abundant fortune, and longevity, embodying auspicious meanings, a rarity among similar pieces. The blue and white colors are vibrant, with clear hierarchical layers of decoration and balanced composition. On the base, the mark “Da Qing Qianlong Nian Zhi” (Made in the Qianlong era of the Great Qing) is inscribed in a distinctive seal script, reminiscent of a certain type of Yongzheng seal script, presumably employed during the early Qianlong period.

清 乾隆

青花缠枝花卉纹铺首尊 高：25.4 厘米

大清乾隆年制（六字三行篆书款）

《清宫内造办处档案》载乾隆三年（1738）六月二十五日，唐英以“宣窑收小青花双环七弦尊”为样本烧制。档案中所载器物即应指本器。乾隆朝伊始，此式首弦纹尊遂成为每年大运瓷器必烧之品类。

是器造型端庄，仿上古青铜器而制，撇口，束颈，丰肩，上饰双兽首衔环，鼓腹渐收至底，高圈足外撇。自口沿而下分绘海浪纹、蕉叶纹、缠枝莲纹、缠枝花卉纹、海水波涛纹和莲瓣纹六层纹饰，肩、腹、腰、胫部之间以七条突起的弦纹分隔，工艺考究，繁而不乱。青花发色纯艳典雅，笔触点染为仿明早期青花之苏麻离青效果，自然灵动。

QING DYNASTY, QIANLONG MARK AND PERIOD

A FINE BLUE AND WHITE "FLORAL" VASE Height: 25.4 cm

Recorded in the *Qing Archives,* Tang Ying fired a vase using the "Xuan kiln small blue and white double-ring seven-string vase" as a model on June 25, 1738. The vase is believed to refer to this piece. From the onset of the Qianlong period, this style of seven-string pattern vases subsequently became a category of porcelain that was fired annually.

This vase has a solemn form, fabricated in imitation of ancient bronze vessels, with a flared mouth, constrained neck, plump shoulders adorned with dual beast-head ring handles. The body tapers down to the base with a high ring foot flaring outward. From the rim downward, it is decorated with six layers of patterns: wave patterns, banana leaf patterns, entwined lotus patterns, entwined floral patterns, sea wave patterns, and lotus petal patterns. The spaces between the shoulders, belly, waist, and base are separated by seven protruding string patterns, demonstrating meticulous craftsmanship in a complex yet orderly fashion. The blue and white hues are pure and elegantly classic, with the brushstrokes dabbing to imitate the effect of early Ming Dynasty blue-and-white porcelain, embodying a natural and lively essence.

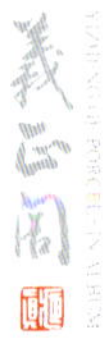

清 乾隆

青花缠枝花卉开光福寿纹抱月瓶 高：24.4厘米

大清乾隆年制（六字三行篆书款）

是器圆口外侈，短颈，扁圆腹，前、后腹部中心凸起桃形开光，附设如意绶带双耳。瓶身以拼接法制成，工艺复杂。瓶口自上而下分绘缠枝灵芝纹、如意纹、缠枝西番莲纹、缠枝莲纹、福寿纹、卷草纹共六层，主题纹饰为缠枝西番莲，桃形开光内绘五枚蟠桃，枝叶垂垂，生机犹存。四周蝠纹围绕，轻灵秀逸，更有寿上加寿之意。底青花书“大清乾隆年制”篆书款。是器造型应是受西亚器物风格影响而烧制，青花发色明艳，笔触点染为仿明早期青花之苏麻离青效果。属清宫每年必备的大运琢器之一。

QING DYNASTY, QIANLONG MARK AND PERIOD

A BLUE-AND-WHITE PEACH "MEDALLION" MOONFLASK

Height: 24.4 cm

This moonflask has a flared round mouth, short neck, and flattened body with peach-shaped medallion, adorned with a pair of ruyi-form handles. Crafted using a patchwork technique, it showcases intricate craftsmanship. It's decorated with six layers of motifs around the mouth: entwined lingzhi, ruyi, entwined lotus, entwined flower, fortune and longevity, and scroll patterns, with the main theme being the entwined lotus. On the peach-shaped medallion, five peaches are painted, surrounded by elegant bat motifs symbolizing fortune and longevity due to the homonym "fu" (happiness) in Chinese. The base bears the seal script marking "Da Qing Qianlong Nian Zhi" (Made during the Qianlong era of the Great Qing) in blue-and-white. Influenced by West Asian styles, the bright blue-and-white color scheme replicates the Samarra Blue (sumali qing) effect from the early Ming Dynasty. This is one of the essential pieces in the imperial palace every year during the Qing Dynasty.

清 乾隆
斗彩团菊纹盖罐 高：11.9 厘米

大清乾隆年制（六字三行篆书款）

是器直颈鼓腹，盖呈扁圆形，整体造型敦实可人。胎体紧致，修胎规整，釉面润泽，颈下、足上一周以青花分两色渲染变形如意云头，云头中心点红、黄彩。腹部主体以斗彩绘团菊纹，团菊上下分布，背景衬托蕉叶，团菊呈品字形分布，其间饰缠枝莲纹，盖面两朵团菊均为红色，盖沿一周绘莲纹，与腹身团菊间莲纹相近。此式莲菊纹罐，其团菊纹与成化瓷器所饰接近，然传世成化器中，并未发现式样相同之品。

QING DYNASTY, QIANLONG MARK AND PERIOD
A DOUCAI "LOTUS AND CHRYSANTHEMUM" JAR AND COVER Height: 11.9 cm

This jar features a straight neck and bulbous body, with a flat circular lid, presenting a robust and pleasing overall form. The body is tightly potted with a smooth surface and lustrous glaze. Around the neck and foot, it is adorned with blue-and-white rendered ruyi cloud-head bands, with the centers of the cloud heads accented in red and yellow. The main body is painted with roundels enclosing pairs of red and yellow blooming chrysanthemum against leafy green grounds, alternating with lotus in red and yellow enamels borne on undulating leafy scrolls. The flat-topped cover is similarly decorated with a chrysanthemum medallion in the center and four leafy lotus adorned on the side. The base is marked with the six-character seal script in underglaze blue reading "Da Qing Qianlong Nian Zhi" (Made during the Qianlong era of the Great Qing). This lotus and chrysanthemum patterned jar, with its tuanju pattern, bears a close resemblance to those on Chenghua porcelain, although no identical pieces have been found among the extant Chenghua pieces.

清 乾隆

暗刻海水绿龙盘

直径：17.8 厘米

大清乾隆年制（六字三行篆书款）

是器口沿微撇，弧腹，圈足。盘心及外壁均饰龙纹，龙纹皆墨线勾写，填透明绿釉，外壁弦纹内暗刻海水鳞波纹。所绘白地暗纹绿龙，骨秀神清，龙体健美，超脱奔放，极富神采。整器纹饰内外相应，情趣陡升，刻工娴熟流畅，所刻行龙苍劲凶猛，气势恢宏，方寸之间犹有排山倒海之势，为清代官窑传统品种。

QING DYNASTY, QIANLONG MARK AND PERIOD

A GREEN-ENAMELED "DRAGON" DISH

Diameter: 17.8 cm

The dish features a gently flaring rim, rounded body, and a ring foot. Both the interior and exterior are adorned with dragon motifs, meticulously outlined in ink with transparent green glaze filling. The exterior's string patterns are subtly incised with sea-wave and scale motifs. The depicted dragons, set against a white background with incised green scales, exhibit a refined skeletal structure, spirited expressions, and robust, elegant forms, embodying a transcendent, vigorous essence that captivates the beholder. The dish's artistic appeal is significantly elevated by the harmonious patterned decorations both within and outside of it, all executed with a smooth flow of adept craftsmanship. The carved dragons exude a ferocious, vigorous energy even though encapsulated a majestic demeanor within the confined space. The base is inscribed in blue underglaze with the six-character seal script mark "Da Qing Qianlong Nian Zhi" (Made during the Qianlong era of the Great Qing), representing a traditional product of the Qing Dynasty official kilns.

清 乾隆

松石绿地粉彩描金宝相花纹茶碗

直径：11.2 厘米

大清乾隆年制（六字三行篆书款）

是器侈口，弧壁，深腹，圈足。内壁洁白匀净无纹饰，外壁以松石绿釉为地，口沿下粉彩绘如意云头纹，腹部饰宝相花纹，其间点缀红蝠口衔“卍”字符，其下缀缠枝结寿桃，寓意福寿万年。近足处饰变形莲瓣纹一周。此器精绝之处在于追摹铜胎掐丝珐琅器之质感，以松石绿釉摹仿铜胎掐丝珐琅之色地，并以金彩画骨，勾勒花纹轮廓线框，带出鎏金掐丝之质感，而卷草上的红、黄、绿三彩质感硬朗深沉，亦为掐丝珐琅常见的颜色，极为写实逼真。

QING DYNASTY, QIANLONG MARK AND PERIOD

A FINE TURQUOISE GROUND FAMILLE ROSE BOWL

Diameter: 11.2cm

This piece possesses a flared rim, curved walls, a deep belly, and a ring foot. The interior wall is clean and smooth without any decoration, while the exterior is coated with a turquoise glaze as the ground color. Below the rim, there is a famille-rose painting of ruyi cloud motifs, and on the belly, a precious scroll motif is adorned. Amidst these motifs, red bats hold the “swastika” symbol in their mouths, below which are intertwined branches holding longevity peaches, symbolizing everlasting fortune and longevity. Near the foot, a row of altered lotus petal motifs encircles the piece. The base is inscribed with “Da Qing Qianlong Nian Zhi” (Made during the Qianlong era of the Great Qing) in seal script with iron red color. The remarkable finesse of this piece lies in its emulation of the texture found in cloisonné enamel wares with copper bodies. The turquoise glaze mimics the color ground of copper-bodied cloisonné enamel, and the gilt outlines delineate the motif contours, bringing forth the texture of gilded cloisonné wire. The robust and rich texture of red, yellow, and green on the scrollwork is also a common coloration found in cloisonné enamel, rendering a highly realistic and vivid aesthetic.

YIZHENG GE PORCELAIN ALBUM

義正閣

清 嘉庆 道光

NQIG DYNASTY,

JIAQING AND DAOGUANG PERIOD

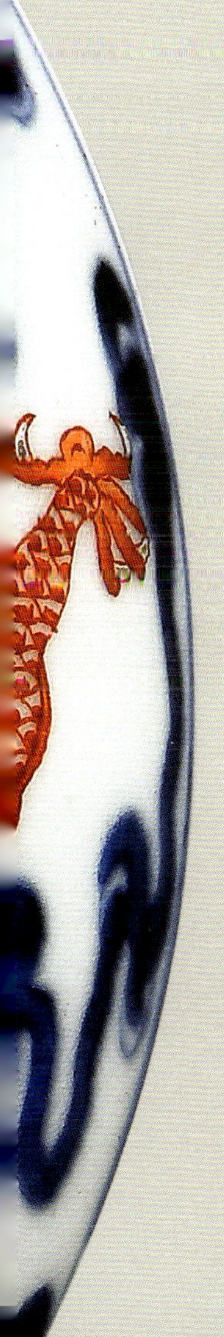

清 嘉庆

青花矾红云龙纹盖盒一对

直径：16 厘米 ×2

大清嘉庆年制（六字三行篆书款）

是器呈扁圆式，盖面以矾红绘制五条威龙，一条居中呈正面龙形，四条盘旋于其周围，威龙凶猛矫健，神态肃穆，身形俱佳，栩栩如生，五龙爪锋利异常，细长尖锐，宛如铁钩，威严之感倍增。盒身亦绘有五条矾红威龙，与盖面交相呼应。群龙之间点缀青花祥云纹，祥云飘浮，深沉浓重，色彩对比明显。

QING DYNASTY, JIAQING MARK AND PERIOD

A RARE PAIR OF BLUE AND WHITE "DRAGON" BOXES WITH COVERS

Diameter: 16 cm×2

This pair of boxes showcases a flat-rounded shape, where the cover is adorned with iron-red painted mighty dragons. A singular dragon is depicted in the center exhibiting a frontal dragon form, encircled by four other dragons swirling around it. These dragons are portrayed with fierce and vigorous demeanors, exuding a sense of solemn majesty. The intricacy in the rendering of their forms is remarkable, bringing them to life in a vivid manner. The claws of the five dragons are notably sharp, long, and pointed, resembling iron hooks, augmenting the awe-inspiring aura of the scene. The body of the boxes also carry the depiction of five iron-red mighty dragons, harmoniously echoing the design on the cover. Among the dragons, blue and white auspicious cloud patterns are interspersed, floating amidst them with a rich and dense appearance, creating a striking contrast in colors. The base is inscribed with "Da Qing Jiaqing Nian Zhi" (Made during the Jiaqing era of the Great Qing) in blue underglaze, written in seal script.

清 嘉庆
珊瑚红地五彩描金婴戏图碗 直径：21 厘米

大清嘉庆年制（六字三行篆书款）

十六子婴戏图碗始见于永乐青花器，至清康熙朝则独创珊瑚红地五彩，并加描金，然其后仅嘉庆一朝承袭烧造，存世稀少。

是器外壁施珊瑚红釉为地，通景以五彩绘庭院婴戏图，松林庭院间，十六童子济济一堂，面庞圆润，神情稚拙可爱，或围缸戏水，或执木偶，或捧瓶而视，呈现热闹欢快之喜庆气氛，其后景色以金彩描绘，清幽雅致，绚丽夺目。全器构图考究，绘画传神，主题祥瑞，风格独具，有百子千孙、多子多福之美好寓意。

敏求精舍旧藏

QING DYNASTY, JIAQING MARK AND PERIOD
A RARE AND FINE CORAL-GROUND FAMILLE-ROSE "BOYS" BOWL Diameter: 21 cm

The depiction of sixteen playful boys on bowls first appeared on Yongle blue-and-white ware. By the Qing Dynasty's Kangxi reign, the unique coral-red ground famille-rose, adorned with gilding, was introduced. However, only during the Jiaqing reign was this style continued, making extant pieces exceptionally rare.

This exquisite bowl exhibits a coral-red glazed exterior, with a lively scene of children at play within a courtyard painted in vibrant famille-rose enamels. Amidst the pine garden, sixteen cherubic children gather, their plump faces exuding innocent charm. Some frolic by a water vat, others hold wooden dolls, while some peer into a jar, creating a merry, festive ambiance. The background is accented with gilded details, adding a touch of quiet elegance amidst the eye-catching splendor. The meticulous composition, lifelike portrayal, auspicious theme, and distinctive style symbolize wishes for abundant offspring and blessings, resonating with the Chinese cultural ideals of prosperity and good fortune. The base is marked with "Da Qing Jiaqing Nian Zhi" (Made during the Qing Jiaqing era of the Great Qing) in seal script.

Collection of Mingqiu Society

清 道光

胭脂红地轧道洋彩开光五谷丰登图碗一对 直径：14.8 厘米 ×2

大清道光年制（六字三行篆书款）

是器为宫碗式样，外壁于胭脂红轧道地上四面开光，内绘博古纹，可见吉磬、如意、宝瓶、四季花卉、鼎、五谷、灯笼等诸式纹样，寓意五谷丰登、四季平安、吉庆有余，至为吉祥。开光间以俯仰折枝莲纹相隔。碗内青花装饰，碗心双圈内绘十字宝杵式花纹，内壁饰宝伞、宝盖等吉祥杂宝。红彩妍美，轧道精工，全器色调鲜艳华贵，装饰效果强烈，具有鲜明的年节喜庆色彩，乃上元节御用佳器。

QING DYNASTY, DAOGUANG MARK AND PERIOD

A FINE PAIR OF RUBY-GROUND FAMILLE-ROSE SGRAFFIATO "LANTERNS" BOWLS Diameter: 14.8 cm×2

This pair of bowls, epitomizing imperial-style from the Daoguang era, showcases a ruby sgraffiato ground adorned with yangcai (foreign colors) embellishments. The exterior reveals meticulously carved medallion on four sides, unveiling exquisite bogu (antique) patterns. These depict auspicious symbols like ruyi (scepter), treasure vase, seasonal florals, ding (ancient vessel), grains, and lanterns, symbolizing "abundant aarvest", "four seasons of peace", and "surplus of joy", embodying profound auspiciousness. The medallion sections are interspersed with elegant lotus motifs. Inside, blue and white porcelain artistry is displayed. The heart of the bowl features a cruciform vajra pattern encased within double rings, while the inner walls are embellished with treasure umbrellas, treasure covers, and various auspicious treasures. The vibrant rouge coloring and superb carving craftsmanship present a palette full of splendor and richness. The decorative vigor of the piece is strong, resonating with the lively celebratory colors of festivities, making it a splendid ceremonial vessel for the Lantern Festival.

清 道光

胭脂红地轧道洋彩开光四季山水纹碗

直径：14.3 厘米

大清道光年制（六字三行篆书款）

是器为宫碗式样，碗内白釉滋润光亮，碗心以洋彩绘宝相花纹，外壁匀施胭脂红釉为地，施以轧道工艺，并以洋彩绘俯仰折枝西番莲纹为饰，富贵华美，锦地上四面开光，内以洋彩绘《春日行旅》《携琴访友》《秋山访寺》《雪夜读书》四图，所绘山水楼台错落有致，层次分明，以不同景物、色调描绘四季景色之变换，追求国画笔墨格调。

QING DYNASTY, DAOGUANG MARK AND PERIOD

A FINE AND RARE RUBY-GROUND FAMILLE-ROSE SGRAFFIATO "LANDSCAPE" BOWL

Diameter: 14.3 cm

This piece is fashioned in a palace bowl style, with a white glaze inside that is rich and luminous. The interior is painted with a stylized octagonal rosette highlighted in gilt. The exterior is evenly covered with a carmine red glaze, featuring sgraffiato technique, and adorned with a downward and upward bending Western Paeonia pattern painted in multi-colour, exuding a sense of wealth and splendor. Four medallions are revealed on the ruby sgraffiato ground, each depicting scholars travelling amidst mountainous wintry landscapes including "spring travel", "visiting friends with a zither", "autumn mountain temple visit", and "reading on a snowy night". The depicted landscapes and architectural structures are well-arranged with clear layers, narrating the changes of the four seasons through different scenes and color tones, aiming to capture the essence of traditional Chinese painting style.

清 道光

蓝地轧道洋彩开光花卉纹碗 直径：15 厘米

大清道光年制（六字三行篆书款）

是器为宫碗式样，碗心青花双圈内饰四组缠枝菊花纹。外壁蓝地剔地锦纹上绘四组折枝扁菊，每组两朵，四组描金开光内均绘各彩菊纹。此式碗肇始于乾隆初年所制洋彩色地四围锦上添花膳碗，工艺复杂，色泽艳丽，视觉效果极为华美，乃重阳节御用佳器。

QING DYNASTY, DAOGUANG MARK AND PERIOD

A RARE BLUE-GROUND FAMILLE-ROSE "MEDALLION" BOWL Diameter: 15 cm

This bowl adopts a palace-style. The interior decorated in cobalt blue with chrysanthemums, daisies and peonies in foliage in the center and four small flowering bushes on the wall. The exterior is decorated with four circular medallions that are outlined in gilt, featuring chrysanthemums in reserve on a pale blue background embellished with an incised sgraffito decoration of floral scrolls. Garlands of flowers and stylized lotuses are interspersed between the medallions. This style of bowl originates from the yangcai colored ground bowls produced during the early Qianlong period, with intricate craftsmanship and vibrant colors rendering a visually extravagant effect, making it a superior imperial choice for the Double Ninth Festival.

清 道光

粉地轧道洋彩开光丹桂玉兔纹碗一对

直径：14.8 厘米 ×2

大清道光年制（六字三行篆书款）

是器为宫碗式样，碗内以青花为饰，碗心绘丹桂玉兔纹，图中丹桂飘香，洞石玲珑，玉兔安恬伏于芳草地中，内壁绘四组青花折枝四季花卉，青花色泽鲜亮明快，笔触清秀可人。外壁粉红地粉彩轧道卷草纹作地，四面开光，各开光之间以缠枝西番莲间隔，各开光内绘粉彩花卉，绘画工致细腻，设色鲜艳华丽，乃中秋节御用佳器。

QING DYNASTY, DAOGUANG MARK AND PERIOD

A FINE PAIR OF PINK-GROUND FAMILLE-ROSE "MEDALLION" BOWLS

Diameter: 14.8 cm×2

This pair of bowls exhibits the palace bowl design, adorned internally with blue-and-white decoration. The interior of both bowls are decorated in underglaze blue with four floral groupings encircling a central medallion which contains a scene of a rabbit in a landscape of trees and rocks, displaying a vibrant and cheerful blue-and-white hue with delicate and appealing brushwork. The exteriors feature four roundels, each containing a different cluster of flowering branches, and flanked by stylized floral sprays reserved on a bright pink sgraffiato ground. The artistry is detailed and delicate, with vivid and glamorous coloration, making this pair an imperial choice for the Mid-Autumn Festival.

清 道光

黄地轧道洋彩开光花卉纹碗

直径：14.7 厘米

大清道光年制（六字三行篆书款）

是器为宫碗式样，外壁于柠檬黄彩上以细密轧道技法装饰，圆形开光四组，内绘粉彩花卉图，开光间以海水托起折枝仙桃万字带为饰，寓意万寿无疆。碗内壁亦以青花绘与外壁类似花卉图案，碗心圆形开光内绘《福山寿海》《灵芝青竹》《万字锦带》等图。全器色彩浓艳，绘工娴熟，乃万寿节御用佳器。

QING DYNASTY, DAOGUANG MARK AND PERIOD

A FINE YELLOW-GROUND FAMILLE-ROSE "MEDALLION" BOWL

Diameter: 14.7 cm

This exquisite bowl is emblematic of the palace bowl style, intricately adorned using a delicate sgraffiato technique on a lemon-yellow glaze on its exterior. The circular "medallions" feature fine Famille-Rose floral motifs, set amid four groups, encapsulated by gilt borders. Between the "medallions", gilt-decorated "swastika" characters and peach branches, symbolic of boundless longevity, are elegantly poised over a stylized sea wave motif, giving a touch of imperial auspiciousness. The interior is similarly adorned with blue-and-white floral motifs, and at the core, a circular "medallion" is beautifully illustrated with themes of blessings and longevity, lingzhi and green bamboo, as well as swastika on a ribbon. The entire piece is rich in color, displaying a mastery of craftsmanship. It is a splendid representation of the imperial wares used during the celebratory feast of the of the Emperor's Birthday.

清 道光

黄地轧道洋彩开光山水纹碗

直径：14.9厘米

大清道光年制（六字三行篆书款）

是器为宫碗式样，碗内施透明白釉，莹润细洁，碗心以粉彩为饰，绘变形宝相花。外壁以黄彩轧道为地，剔勾细腻精致，黄彩娇嫩华贵。其上绘勾连花卉，借鉴了西洋绘画技法，敷以各色粉彩，规整夺目。四面圆形开光，开光处绘山水人物图，为《携琴访友》《踏雪寻梅》《寒江独钓》《楼阁静思》四图。

QING DYNASTY, DAOGUANG MARK AND PERIOD

YELLOW-GROUND FAMILLE-ROSE "MEDALLION" BOWL

Diameter: 14.9 cm

This artifact exemplifies a palace-style bowl. The interior of the bowl is applied with a transparent white glaze, presenting a smooth, fine, and glossy finish. The center of the bowl is adorned with fencai (famille rose) enamels depicting a stylized flower with eight ruyi-tipped petals. The exterior wall features a yellow ground with a graffito technique, exhibiting delicate and exquisite incised lines, rendering a tender and luxurious appearance to the yellow color. The external decoration includes connecting flower motifs, which borrow from Western painting techniques, applied with various colored fencai enamels, presenting a neat and eye-catching arrangement. Four circular medallions are crafted on the outer surface, within which scenes of landscapes and figures are finely painted to signify different themes including carrying zither to visit a friend, treading snow in search of plums, fishing alone on a cold river, and quiet contemplation in a tower.

清 道光

蓝地轧道洋彩牛郎织女图碗 直径：14.8厘米

大清道光年制（六字三行篆书款）

是器为宫碗式样，内以青花绘“牛郎织女鹊桥相会”图，鹊鸟翩飞，祥云缭绕，牛郎织女相顾脉脉，缱绻情深。内壁对称绘四组祥云纹，各以展翅鹊鸟相隔。外壁饰蓝釉轧道纹为地，轧道精致细密，似锦铺就之感，四开光内分别绘牛郎、织女、燃香、起居四图，绘画生动，栩栩如生，开光间以祥云相隔。此类御用膳碗创烧于乾隆时期，专为七夕而设，并为道光朝所沿用。

QING DYNASTY, DAOGUANG MARK AND PERIOD

A FINE BLUE-GROUND FAMILLE-ROSE “MEDALLION” BOWL

Diameter: 14.8 cm

This exquisite piece is a palace-style bowl from the Daoguang era of the Qing Dynasty, embodying a rich cultural narrative through its intricate designs. The interior features underglaze blue porcelain artwork depicting the legendary tale of the Cowherd and the Weaver Girl meeting on the magpie bridge, a story celebrated on Qixi Festival, the Chinese Valentine’s Day. The scene is lively with magpies fluttering amidst auspicious clouds, while the Cowherd and Weaver Girl share a tender, loving gaze, embodying their deep, intertwined emotions. The interior rim displays symmetrically painted auspicious cloud motifs, each separated by a soaring magpie. It showcases four medallions, each illustrating distinct scenes of the Cowherd, Weaver Girl, incense burning, and daily life, bringing the artwork to life with a vivid, lifelike touch. Between the medallions, auspicious clouds serve as delicate separators on blue sgraffiato ground. This type of imperial dining bowl, designed specifically for the Qixi Festival, originated in the Qianlong period and continued to be cherished during the Daoguang reign.

清 道光

胭脂红地轧道洋彩开光花果纹碗 直径：14.5厘米

大清道光年制（六字三行篆书款）

是器为宫碗式样，碗心绘青花花篮及灵符纹，内壁等距绘四组青花折枝花果，外壁以胭脂红彩为地，其上满饰繁密的轧道卷草纹，等距排列之四开光内绘以各种粉彩花果，开光间均饰西番莲纹相隔。整器工艺繁复，色泽鲜丽，装饰效果强烈，乃端阳节御用佳器。

QING DYNASTY, DAOGUANG MARK AND PERIOD

A VERY FINE RUBY-GROUND GRAFFIATO "MEDALLION" BOWL Diameter: 14.5 cm

This artifact embodies the style of an imperial bowl. The interior is painted in cobalt blue with a floral basket and talisman motif surrounded by four sets of floral branches and mugwort leaves (a plant used during Dragon Boat Festival as tradition). Four equidistant medallions, each showcasing a variety of pastel-colored fruits and flowers, are carefully arranged on the exterior, surrounded by lotus motifs on a ruby sgraffiato ground. The craftsmanship of this piece is intricate, showcasing vivid colors and robust decorative effects, making it a fine imperial ware for the Dragon Boat Festival celebration.

002
明永乐
青花缠枝花卉纹花口盘

MING DYNASTY,
YONGLE PERIOD
A BLUE AND WHITE
BARBED "FLORAL" PLATE

006
明宣德
青花折枝花果纹葵口碗

MING DYNASTY,
XUANDE MARK AND PERIOD
A BLUE AND WHITE LOBED
"FRUIT AND FLOWER" BOWL

008
明宣德
青花折枝花果纹大碗

MING DYNASTY,
XUANDE MARK AND PERIOD
A VERY RARE BLUE AND
WHITE "FRUIT" BOWL

010
明宣德
青花双莲瓣缠枝莲纹碗

MING DYNASTY,
XUANDE MARK AND PERIOD
A BLUE AND WHITE LOTUS BOWL

016

清康熙
五彩《望月图》诗文笔筒

QING DYNASTY,
KANGXI PERIOD
AN EXTRAORDINARY,
FINE AND LARGE INSCRIBED
FAMILLE VERTE BRUSHPOT

020

清康熙
釉里红加五彩花卉纹
苹果尊

QING DYNASTY,
KANGXI MARK AND PERIOD
A RARE AND EXCEPTIONAL
COPPER-RED AND
FAMILLE VERTE "ROSE" VASE

022

清康熙
釉里红加五彩花卉纹
马蹄尊

QING DYNASTY,
KANGXI MARK AND PERIOD
A FINE AND RARE ENAMELLED
AND COPPER-RED DECORATED
WATER POT, HORSESHOE VASE

026

清康熙
冬青釉浅浮雕
祥云纹马蹄式水盂

QING DYNASTY,
KANGXI MARK AND PERIOD
A FINE CARVED
CELADON-GLAZED
"CLOUD" WATER POT

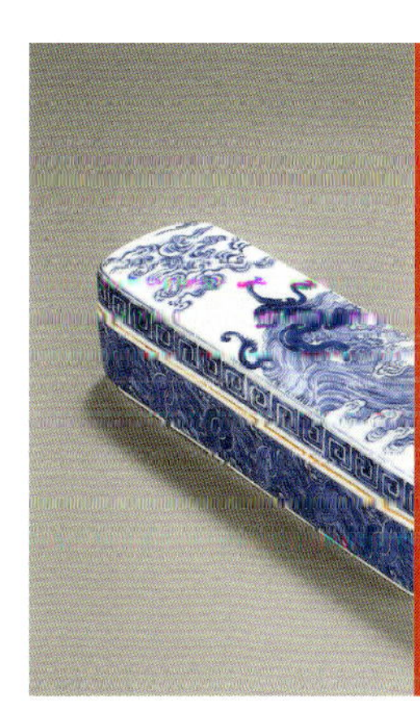

028

清康熙
青花海水云龙纹文具盒

QING DYNASTY,
KANGXI PERIOD
A RARE BLUE AND WHITE
"DRAGON" CALLIGRAPHY
BOX WITH COVER

030

清康熙
青花五彩
八月佳花花神杯

QING DYNASTY,
KANGXI MARK AND PERIOD
A WUCAI "OSMANTHUS"
MONTHLY CUP

032

清康熙
青花五彩
六月荷花花神杯

QING DYNASTY,
KANGXI MARK AND PERIOD
A RARE WUCAI "LOTUS"
MONTHLY CUP

034

清康熙
珊瑚红地瓷胎画
珐琅九秋图宫碗

QING DYNASTY,
KANGXI MARK AND PERIOD
A FINE AND RARE CORAL-
GROUND FAMILLE-
VERTE FLORAL BOWL

036

清康熙
青花斗绿彩赶珠
云龙纹大盘

QING DYNASTY,
KANGXI MARK AND PERIOD
A FINE AND RARE
GREEN-ENAMELLED
"DRAGON" DISH

040

清雍正
斗彩鸡缸杯

QING DYNASTY,
YONGZHENG MARK AND PERIOD
A RARE DOUCAI CHICKEN CUP

044

清雍正
斗彩团菊纹杯

QING DYNASTY,
YONGZHENG MARK AND PERIOD
A FINE DOUCAI
"CHRYSANTHEMUM
MEDALLION" WINE CUP

046

清雍正
斗彩暗八仙纹碗

QING DYNASTY,
YONGZHENG MARK AND PERIO
A FINE DOUCAI
"ANBAXIAN" BOWL

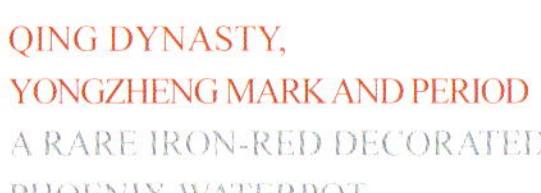

048

清雍正
矾红夔凤纹水盂

QING DYNASTY,
YONGZHENG MARK AND PERIOD
A RARE IRON-RED DECORATED
PHOENIX WATERPOT

050

清雍正
柠檬黄釉茶圆一对

QING DYNASTY,
YONGZHENG MARK AND PERIOD
A PAIR OF VERY RARE
YELLOW GLAZE BOWLS

052

清雍正
松石绿釉葵式茶碗一对

QING DYNASTY,
YONGZHENG MARK AND PERIC
A VERY RARE PAIR OF
MOULDED TURQUOISE-
ENAMELLED MALLOW-
FORM TEA BOWLS

056

清雍正
霁红釉小瓶

QING DYNASTY,
YONGZHENG MARK AND PERIOD
A RARE COPPER-RED
GLAZED VASE

060

清雍正
霁蓝釉胆瓶一对

QING DYNASTY,
YONGZHENG MARK AND PERIOD
A PAIR OF VERY RARE
BOTTLE VASES WITH
BLUE GLAZE

062

清雍正
斗彩缠枝
西番莲纹长颈瓶

QING DYNASTY,
YONGZHENG MARK AND PERIC
A VERY RARE DOUCAI VASE
WITH ENTWINED BRANCHE-
AND LOTUS DESIGN

066

清雍正
窑变釉双耳盘口瓶

QING DYNASTY,
YONGZHENG MARK AND PERIOD
A VERY RARE VASE
WITH FLAMBÉ GLAZE

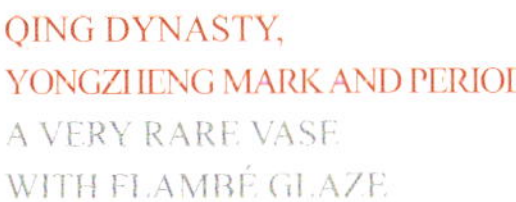

070

清雍正
洒蓝地白花缠枝
花卉纹盘

QING DYNASTY,
YONGZHENG MARK AND PERIOD
A RARE REVERSE-
DECORATED POWDER-
BLUE "GARDENIA" DISH

072

清雍正
青花加矾红
折枝宝相花纹杯

QING DYNASTY,
YONGZHENG MARK AND PERIOD
A FINE UNDERGLAZE-
BLUE AND IRON-RED
"LOTUS" CUP

074

清雍正
斗彩菊花捧寿纹盘

QING DYNASTY,
YONGZHENG MARK AND PERIOD
A FINE DOUCAI
CHRYSANTHEMUM AND
LONGEVITY PATTERN PLATE

076

清雍正
斗彩海屋添筹图盘

QING DYNASTY,
YONGZHENG MARK AND PERIOD
A RARE DOUCAI
"IMMORTALS" DISH

078

清雍正
斗彩如意云龙纹盘

QING DYNASTY,
YONGZHENG MARK AND PERIOD
A VERY RARE DOUCAI
"DRAGON" DISH

080

清雍正
斗彩绿龙纹盘

QING DYNASTY,
YONGZHENG MARK AND PERIOD
A FINE AND RARE
UNDERGLAZE-BLUE AND
GREEN-ENAMELLED
"DRAGON" DISH

082

清雍正
釉里红三鱼纹盘一对

QING DYNASTY,
YONGZHENG MARK AND PERIOD
A FINE PAIR OF COPPER-
RED DECORATED
"THREE-FISH" DISHES

086

清乾隆
青花釉里红
狮滚绣球纹尊

QING DYNASTY,
QIANLONG MARK AND PERIOD
A FINE AND VERY RARE
UNDERGLAZE-BLUE AND
COPPER-RED "LION" VASE

090

清乾隆
青花缠枝番莲
寿字纹如意尊

QING DYNASTY,
QIANLONG MARK AND PERIOD
A FINE AND VERY RARE
BLUE-AND-WHITE
DOUBLE-GOURD VASE

094

清乾隆
青花双龙捧寿纹
如意耳葫芦扁瓶一对

QING DYNASTY,
QIANLONG MARK AND PERIOD
A PAIR OF BLUE AND
WHITE DRAGON
DOUBLE-GOURD VASES

096

清乾隆
粉彩云龙纹笔

QING DYNASTY,
QIANLONG MARK AND PERIOD
A FINE AND RARE FAMILLE-
ROSE "DRAGON" BRUSH

098

清乾隆
釉里红喜上眉梢图
如意耳抱月瓶

QING DYNASTY,
QIANLONG MARK AND PERIOD
A RARE UNDERGLAZE-RED
"MAGPIE AND PRUNUS"
MOONFLASK

100

清乾隆
胭脂红地洋彩轧道
锦上添花纹贯耳扁瓶

QING DYNASTY,
QIANLONG MARK AND PERIOD
A YANGCAI RUBY-GROUND
SGRAFFITO LOTUS VASE

102

清乾隆
松绿地粉彩缠枝莲纹
五子登科包袱瓶

QING DYNASTY,
QIANLONG MARK AND PERIOI
A VERY RARE PINE TURQUOI
GROUND FAMILLE ROSE
"FIVE SCHOLARS ATTAINING
SCHOLARLY HONORS"
POUCH-SHAPED VASE

106

清乾隆
粉彩仿掐丝珐琅
番莲福寿纹双龙耳瓶

QING DYNASTY,
QIANLONG PERIOD
A VERY RARE FAMILLE-
ROSE CLOISONNE-IMITATION
BOTTLE VASE

108

清乾隆
仿雕漆珊瑚红地描金
瑞蝠穿云游龙纹帽架

QING DYNASTY,
QIANLONG PERIOD
A VERY RARE IMITATION-
LACQUER "DRAGON"
PORCELAIN HAT STAND

110

清乾隆
粉青釉刻螭龙纹
盘口纸槌瓶

QING DYNASTY,
QIANLONG MARK AND PERIOI
A CELADON GLAZE "DRAGO
MALLET SHAPE VASE

112

清乾隆
粉青釉弦纹高足杯

QING DYNASTY,
QIANLONG MARK AND PERIOD
A FINE STEMBOWL WITH
PALE BLUISH-GREEN
CELADON GLAZE

114

清乾隆
仿汝釉出戟花觚

QING DYNASTY,
QIANLONG MARK AND PERIOD
A FINE RU-TYPE VASE, HUAGU

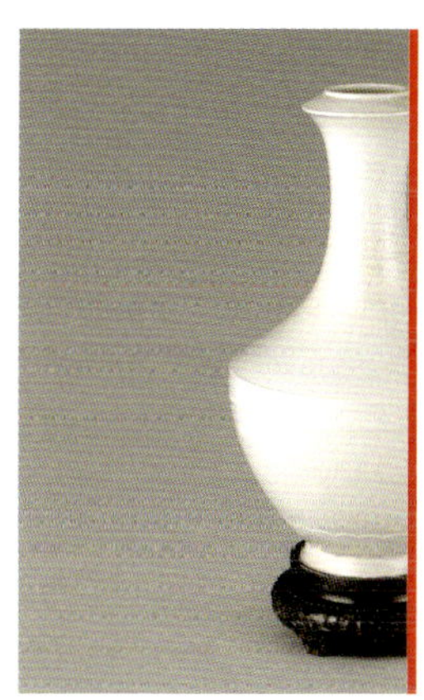

116

清乾隆
浆胎仿定釉
暗刻兽面纹盖碗尊

QING DYNASTY,
QIANLONG MARK AND PERIOD
A FINE AND RARE
CREAMY-WHITE GLAZED
SOFT-PASTE VASE

118

清乾隆
冬青釉刻缠枝
牡丹纹长颈瓶

QING DYNASTY,
QIANLONG MARK AND PERIOD
A RARE AND FINE CELADON
ENAMELED PORCELAIN
VASE WITH
MOLDED DECORATION

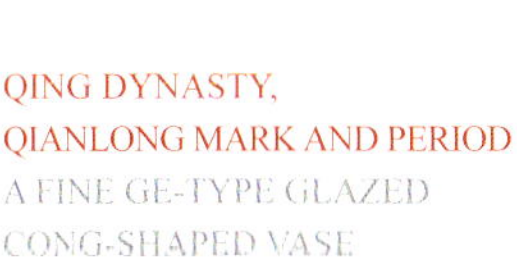

120

清乾隆
仿官釉八卦琮式瓶

QING DYNASTY,
QIANLONG MARK AND PERIOD
A FINE GE-TYPE GLAZED
CONG-SHAPED VASE

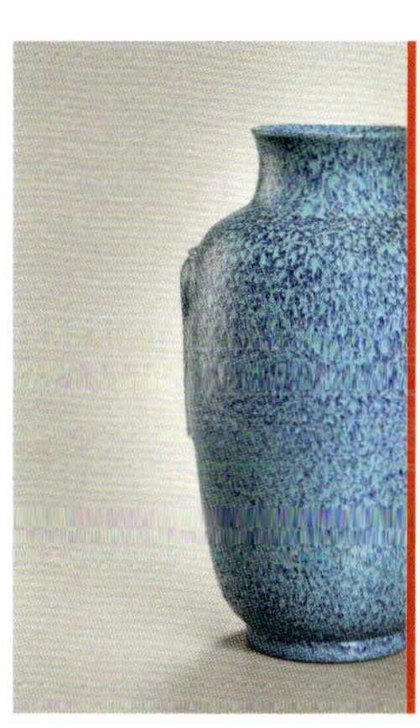

122

清乾隆
炉钧釉灯笼瓶

QING DYNASTY,
QIANLONG MARK AND PERIOD
A ROBIN'S-EGG BLUE GLAZED
LANTERN VASE

124

清乾隆
青花八吉祥纹
双龙耳抱月瓶

QING DYNASTY,
QIANLONG MARK AND PERIOD
A SUPERB LARGE MING-
STYLE BLUE AND WHITE
"BAJIXIANG" MOONFLASK

128

清乾隆
青花折枝花卉纹六方瓶

QING DYNASTY,
QIANLONG MARK AND PERIOD
AN EXCEPTIONALLY FINE
AND MAGNIFICENT
BLUE AND WHITE "SANDUO"
HEXAGONAL VASE

132

清乾隆
青花缠枝西番莲
团寿纹六方贯耳瓶

QING DYNASTY,
QIANLONG MARK AND PERIOD
A FINE BLUE-AND-WHITE
"LOTUS SCROLL"
HEXAGONAL VASE

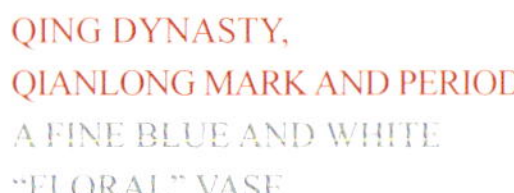

134

清乾隆
青花缠枝花卉纹铺首尊

QING DYNASTY,
QIANLONG MARK AND PERIOD
A FINE BLUE AND WHITE
"FLORAL" VASE

136

清乾隆
青花缠枝花卉
开光福寿纹抱月瓶

QING DYNASTY,
QIANLONG MARK AND PERIOD
A BLUE-AND-WHITE PEACH
"MEDALLION" MOONFLASK

138

清乾隆
斗彩团菊纹盖罐

QING DYNASTY,
QIANLONG MARK AND PERIOD
A DOUCAI "LOTUS AND
CHRYSANTHEMUM" JAR
AND COVER

140

清乾隆
暗刻海水绿龙盘

QING DYNASTY,
QIANLONG MARK AND PERIOD
A GREEN-ENAMELED
"DRAGON" DISH

142

清乾隆
松石绿地粉彩
描金宝相花纹茶碗

QING DYNASTY,
QIANLONG MARK AND PERIOD
A FINE TURQUOISE GROUND
FAMILLE ROSE BOWL

146

清嘉庆
青花矾红云龙纹
盖盒一对

QING DYNASTY,
JIAQING MARK AND PERIOD
A RARE PAIR OF BLUE AND
WHITE "DRAGON" BOXES
WITH COVERS

148

清嘉庆
珊瑚红地五彩描金
婴戏图碗

QING DYNASTY,
JIAQING MARK AND PERIOD
A RARE AND FINE CORAL-
GROUND FAMILLE-
ROSE "BOYS" BOWL

150

清道光
胭脂红地轧道洋彩
开光五谷丰登图碗一对

QING DYNASTY,
DAOGUANG MARK AND PERIOD
A FINE PAIR OF RUBY-GROUND
FAMILLE-ROSE SGRAFFIATO
"LANTERNS" BOWLS

152

清道光
胭脂红地轧道
洋彩开光四季山水纹碗

QING DYNASTY,
DAOGUANG MARK AND PERIOD
A FINE AND RARE RUBY-
GROUND FAMILLE-ROSE
SGRAFFIATO
"LANDSCAPE" BOWL

154

清道光
蓝地轧道洋彩
开光花卉纹碗

QING DYNASTY,
DAOGUANG MARK AND PERIOD
A RARE BLUE GROUND
FAMILLE-ROSE
"MEDALLION" BOWL

156

清道光
粉地轧道洋彩
开光丹桂玉兔纹碗一对

QING DYNASTY,
DAOGUANG MARK AND PERIOD
A FINE PAIR OF PINK-
GROUND FAMILLE-ROSE
"MEDALLION" BOWLS

158

清道光
黄地轧道洋彩
开光花卉纹碗

QING DYNASTY,
DAOGUANG MARK AND PERIOD
A FINE YELLOW-GROUND
FAMILLE-ROSE
"MEDALLION" BOWL

160

清道光
黄地轧道洋彩
开光山水纹碗

QING DYNASTY,
DAOGUANG MARK AND PERIOD
YELLOW-GROUND
FAMILLE-ROSE
"MEDALLION" BOWL

162

清道光
蓝地轧道洋彩
牛郎织女图碗

QING DYNASTY,
DAOGUANG MARK AND PERIOD
A FINE BLUE-GROUND
FAMILLE-ROSE
'MEDALLION' BOWL

164

清道光
胭脂红地轧道洋彩
开光花果纹碗

QING DYNASTY,
DAOGUANG MARK AND PERIOD
A VERY FINE RUBY-
GROUND GRAFFIATO
"MEDALLION" BOWL

图书在版编目（CIP）数据

义正阁藏瓷 / 义正阁主编．-- 杭州：西泠印社出版社，2024.4
ISBN 978-7-5508-4478-0

Ⅰ．①义… Ⅱ．①义… Ⅲ．①瓷器（考古）－中国－明清时代－图集 Ⅳ．① K876.32

中国国家版本馆 CIP 数据核字 (2024) 第 070267 号

義正閣·藏瓷

義正閣 主 编

责任编辑	谭贞寅	策　　划	董　量
装帧设计	袁　正	书法诗文	陆晞明
责任校对	李寒晴	书词撰写	焦　傲
责任出版	冯斌强	翻　　译	禄泽阳
摄　　影	山古影像工作室		

出版发行　西泠印社出版社
（杭州市西湖文化广场 32 号 E 座 5 楼　邮政编码：310014）
经　　销　全国新华书店
制版印刷　上海雅昌艺术印刷有限公司
开　　本　787mm × 1092mm　1/8
字　　数　120 千
印　　张　24
印　　数　001—400
版　　次　2024 年 4 月第 1 版 第 1 次印刷

书　　号　ISBN 978-7-5508-4478-0
定　　价　800.00 元

版权所有　翻印必究　印制差错　负责调换

西泠印社出版社发行部联系方式：（0571）87243079

图录作品所涉朝代年表

Chronologg of Chinese Dynasties

元　朝	**Yuan Dynasty**	**1206—1368**
明　朝	**Ming Dynasty**	**1368—1644**
洪　武	Hongwu	1368—1398
建　文	Jianwen	1399—1402
永　乐	Yongle	1403—1424
洪　熙	Hongxi	1425
宣　德	Xuande	1426—1435
正　统	Zhengtong	1436—1449
景　泰	Jingtai	1450—1456
天　顺	Tianshun	1457—1464
成　化	Chenghua	1465—1487
弘　治	Hongzhi	1488—1505
正　德	Zhengde	1506—1521
嘉　靖	Jiajing	1522—1567
隆　庆	Longqing	1567—1572
万　历	Wanli	1573—1620
泰　昌	Taichang	1620
天　启	Tianqi	1621—1627
崇　祯	Chongzhen	1628—1644
清　朝	**Qing Dynasty**	**1616—1911**
天　命	Tianming	1616—1626
天　聪	Tiancong	1627—1636
崇　德	Chongde	1636—1643
顺　治	Shunzhi	1644—1661
康　熙	Kangxi	1662—1722
雍　正	Yongzheng	1723—1735
乾　隆	Qianlong	1736—1795
嘉　庆	Jiaqing	1796—1820
道　光	Daoguang	1821—1850
咸　丰	Xianfeng	1851—1861
同　治	Tongzhi	1862—1874
光　绪	Guangxu	1875—1908
宣　统	Xuantong	1909—1911